Living On the Front Lines

By Debi Hirtler

Living On the Front Lines
Debi Hirtler

ISBN-13:978-1721991204

ISBN-10:1721991204

Cover Design: Marco Papousek
Editor: Linda Meyer

A portion of the proceeds from this book go to support
impoverished children in Brazil.

First edition 2018.
Printed in the United States of America.

Table of Contents

Acknowledgments

The very first person I would like to thank is my wonderful Lord Jesus, without whom I would not have had the wonderful victories that I share in this book.

I also want to thank my best friend and husband, Reinhard Hirtler, who has helped me in so many ways, by reading the manuscript and giving his godly and knowledgeable advice, and also just being there for me and helping me in all of my weaknesses over these past thirty-one plus years. His example and faithfulness to the Lord is the greatest inspiration of my life. It has been such a privilege being married to him.

I would also like to thank Damaris and Esther who were the first ones to tell me that I should write this book, over twenty years ago! They were children then, and they have both grown into such wonderful and beautiful women.

Pastor Lúcia (from São Paulo) has been a constant voice reminding me every time she saw me that I needed to get this book done. Now you can rest in knowing that I took to heart all the gentle reminding and have finished the work. Thank you.

Thank you too Pastor Antonio in England and Chris in Colorado who were used by the Lord to bring specific words concerning the writing of this book, even if they were unaware of it at the time.

Special thanks to my new daughter in the faith, Karina, who translated this book into Portuguese for me. I trust her completely and utterly and know that she did an amazing job.

And my dear and special friend Linda who agreed to help me by editing the English version; even though we are far apart I still feel the closeness we shared so many years ago and every time we can be together. Thank you for your friendship. I treasure it greatly.

I want to also thank my sons, just because they are my sons and they are wonderful and I love them and are proud of the men they have become.

I would also like to thank all those who

call me "Mom" in Brazil, Austria, USA, England, Poland or wherever you are. I am so privileged to have this title for so many wonderful sons and daughters in the Lord.

The Old Me

Chapter 1 – Family Stuff
Growing up in Los Angeles

In actuality I am not a native-born Californian because I was born in a small town in Pennsylvania. My family moved out to California when I was three years old and my sister, my only sibling, was six months old. The whole rest of our family, grandparents, cousins, aunts and uncles were still in Pennsylvania, so we grew up isolated from a larger family group. It was just the four of us, on our own.

Los Angeles was actually a very scary place for a kid to grow up. Even then, in the late 1960's and early 1970's Los Angeles was a very dangerous place. There were gangs everywhere in downtown L.A. You never went there after dark unless it was absolutely necessary, which it never was for me. Besides, we didn't technically live in the city of Los Angeles, but in a city suburb within LA County, so there was never any need for me to be anywhere near downtown L.A.

Being white was also a disadvantage even then. The majority race then (even more so now) was the Hispanics, which is basically anybody in the States who speaks Spanish, which includes, Mexican, Cuban, Puerto Rican, Chilean, Guatemalan etc. The black community was the second majority, with whites being in the minority. In our neighborhood we whites were called *surfers,* even if we had never surfed a day in our lives.

I took three years of Spanish in High School so I could know if someone near me was talking about me, which the Hispanic men tended to do a lot about any woman near them. One time a Mexican man was talking about me and I knew it, even though I had no clue *what* he was saying about me. I just glared at him. He looked at me and said, in broken English, *"You speak Spanish?"* I said, *"Yes."* So he stopped talking about me because he didn't know exactly how much I understood. The Spanish classes paid off for me that day.

I can still vividly remember when one day my Spanish teacher came into our classroom and started talking really weirdly. He then informed us that he was speaking German, and that he was also the German teacher at the school. He wanted to know if any of us wanted to sign up for his German class. It sounded *way* too difficult, so I remember thinking, *"I will never learn that language."* Little did I know then that German would, in fact, become my second language about twenty-plus years later.

In junior high school (or middle school in some parts of the country), when I was about fourteen or fifteen years old, some Mexican girl got it in her head that I had called her some name, which I never did. For the following two years she chased me home from school almost every day, which was about an hour's walk away. She would regularly verbally threaten me on the school grounds. I should mention here that she outweighed me by at least double my body weight. I had a real fear that if she ever caught me, all she had to do was get me on the ground and sit on me and it would literally kill me by suffocation because of her weight alone.

One particular day she called me over to her again at school. She was with some of her friends and informed me that after school that day, some girls from Los Angeles High School would be waiting for me to *"kick my butt"*, as she put it, which meant to beat me up very badly.

I need to mention here that Los Angeles High School was known at that time for its gang violence. For some strange reason, I suddenly had enough of her threats and just said very calmly, "*Thanks for the warning.*" I then calmly walked away from her. She got very angry at my composed reply. As I was walking away from her, she yelled after me, "*Did you hear what I said?*" I turned back to her and said, "*Yes. Thank you,*" and showed her no more fear, which had accompanied all the other threats in the past.

I really expected to be beaten up badly after leaving school that day or the next, or sometime that week. But to my great surprise, nobody was waiting for me; it was all empty threats just to scare me. And from that day onward she never bothered me again. Her main motivator, fear, was gone, so the threats lost their power over me. Gee, doesn't *that* sound like a Bible verse? (1 Peter 5:8)

> ("*Be sober; be vigilant; because your adversary the devil walks about like a roaring lion, seeking whom he may devour.*")

Empty threats…

Moving Along

For some strange reason, (which is a secret my mother took to the grave with her) after my dad left, my mom, sister and I moved to a different house or apartment about every nine to twelve months. Once, many years later, I asked my mother why we had always moved around so much, but she never gave me an answer. This was actually quite a normal response for her, as she was not a very good communicator when it came to her own family. It seems she did not appear to have that problem with any of her other relationships. To this day I still have no idea why we moved so much.

My best guess about the reason was that she couldn't afford the rent of the previous place or that we had gotten evicted and had to move. When we did move it was not with a moving company. My mother hired a truck, which after I got a driver's license, I usually drove, and usually just the three of us (Mom, Sue and I) picked up all the furniture and boxes and loaded and unloaded them all. Needless to say, I was very strong when I was younger. In my teenage years some of my male friends would also come over and help us.

Little Dot Grows Up

My Mother's name was Dorothy, but she went by the name Dottie, except in her own family; they just called her Dot. She was born and reared in the eastern part of Pennsylvania, in the mountains. She moved to the western part of the State when she was in her late teens or early twenties. She met my dad there soon after that, and she got married when she was twenty-two. Apparently, I was already on the way at that time.

Her father died in a tragic accident at his workplace when she was very young. He supposedly had just been told by a friend that his wife was having an affair, and that he should go home to check. When he did go home he caught her with another man. The next day he had the fatal accident at work. My grandmother remarried about a year later to a different man than the one who was there when her husband came home. Soon afterward she had a baby boy. My mom already had two younger brothers and then had a half-brother from her step-father.

According to my mom, she didn't have

much of a childhood. Because she was the only girl in the family, she had to do all the cleaning, cooking, washing, ironing and taking care of the new baby. I imagine it was one of the primary reasons she left home as soon as she could. She did say that she wanted to join the Navy when she was younger, but her mother would not let her. It could have been one thing that attracted her to my father who was an ex-Marine.

My maternal grandmother was not a very nice woman. She never really showed any tenderness or love in any physical or verbal way, neither toward my mother nor toward her grandchildren, on the rare occasions when we saw her. I imagine that was one of the reasons it was seemingly impossible for my mother to show any physical signs of affection toward her own children.

I remember one time being in a women's conference in Austria and there was an altar call to come forward to forgive our mothers for past things. I thought I had resolved my mother issues at that point, but I felt I should go forward anyway. While I was standing at the front, someone came and put their arms around me and hugged me from behind. I never saw who it was but it evoked the thought, "*Did my mother ever hug me?*" I tried very hard to remember a time she ever did outside of airports, greetings or hospital visits of some sort. I couldn't remember one single time she ever did hug me, and I burst into sobs.

I was eight and my sister was six when my father left us. My mom had to go out and get a job, which left me in charge of my little sister. I remember feeling totally overwhelmed by the burden of it all. Later Mom had to work two jobs just to try to make ends meet. That usually meant the rent and utilities were paid, and she had money for gas, but nothing was left for food. My sister and I were always alone at home and always hungry. There were many days that our only "dinner" was a plain piece of white bread with nothing to put on it. My sister and I tried to get our mother to go get government assistance for food but she was very proud. After a few years she finally broke down and applied for help. The agency said she earned too much money and they refused her any assistance.

Many decades later, after some crisis happened in my life, I went for a few sessions of Christian counseling. During the course of that counseling the Holy Spirit revealed to me that the reason I always felt overwhelmed in circumstances that required me taking responsibility originated when my mom went to work and left me in charge of everything, at eight years of age. After speaking out forgiveness and asking the Holy Spirit to heal my wounded heart, all the feelings of being overwhelmed left and have never come back.

Even though I didn't realize it at the time the Lord was watching over me and taking care of me. *"A father of the fatherless, a defender of widows, is God in His holy habitation."(Psalm 68:5).*

Little Jackie, Big Jack

Little Jackie's parents divorced when he was young (I don't actually know how old he was). One day when little Jackie was about 13 years old he went to visit his father and step-mother. His parents had been divorced for a number of years at that point. When he got there his father was not home and his step-mother was cleaning up something that had broken. His step-mother told him that she had just broken something, but he did not think much of it.

When his father came home, his step-mother said that little Jackie was to blame for breaking the object. His father punished him for breaking it, even though Jackie tried to tell his father that it was his step-mother who had done it.

After that day Jackie left and never returned to visit his father again. He was so angry with him, in fact, that for the next thirty years he would not speak one word to his own father. Then little Jackie grew up and became Jack and joined the United States Marines Corps. He went to Korea to fight, but on the very first weekend in Korea was shot in the legs and was sent home.

Until the day he died he had pain in his legs and often had to take pain killers, but also used alcohol to deaden the pain. Sometimes he used a combination of both. He was angry all the time and got into many fights in bars, where he spent most of his time. He also spent many nights in jail. He started having heart problems, partly because of his lifestyle, but I am convinced partly because of his lack of forgiveness and lack of honor for his father.

With all that anger inside of him it also sometimes came out against women, starting with my mother. He beat her a few times. One time she even had to go to the hospital. There were other women after her, including my step-mother who blamed my mom whenever my dad hit her. He never hit my sister or me in anger or when he was drunk, though, but he did discipline us when we did something wrong (before he left). We usually got to choose, if we wanted a belt or his hand to our bottom. I always chose the belt because his hands were much more painful. Unfortunately, he also never said *"I love you"*, at least not to me, except when he was drunk.

He was my father. I loved him very much, even though I rarely saw him, and he had caused my mother, my sister and me much emotional pain. I wanted to be with him but was never allowed to be. Many years after he left my mom he finally remarried. I then gained a step-sister named Debbie and a step-brother named Chris, who also had a violent temper and ended up in a mental institution for a time. My step-sister was pregnant and had a baby before she was seventeen years old. I think she lived with my dad and step-mother for a while.

My dad made three suicide attempts. I was present just after two of them occurred and during the third one. In the first one, he was at a bar and took a handful of sleeping pills. He blocked the phone so nobody could call an ambulance. As soon as he passed out, they called the ambulance and the paramedics came and got him. They took him to the hospital and pumped out his stomach, so he survived. I just happened to call the bar after they had called the ambulance. When I finally got to the hospital, he was tied to the bed and awake. He was very angry. He was yelling for me to untie the restraints, but I was afraid to. I had no idea what he intended to do. In my confusion and fear, I just left him there and quickly left the hospital. I was sixteen years old at the time.

The second attempt was actually a week before I contacted him again. He had gone outside in the alley behind a bar and tried to shoot himself in the heart with a small pistol. My step-mother was with him at the time, and she grabbed his hand just as the gun went off. The bullet lodged in his shoulder. He left it there for a week! When I happened to call him, he asked me if I had a car, and if I would take him to the hospital to get a bullet removed. When we got to the hospital and the staff found out that he had a bullet wound, they took him to the back immediately. I did not know if I would see him again or if they would lock him away. He did come out some hours later. I was still there waiting for him.

The third attempt happened when my girlfriend and I were on our way to a drive-in movie theater to watch a film. For some reason I asked her if we could stop by my dad's apartment on the way to the movie. He was drunk (as he was most days) and depressed when we got there. After a few minutes he took a can of lighter fluid for a cigarette lighter, and started squirting it all over the apartment, the sofa, chairs, carpet, etc. Then he lit a match. At that point my girlfriend grabbed my hand and dragged me out of there, and she took me to the movie. To this day I have no idea what film we watched. I was only wondering if my dad was alive or dead. Afterwards I asked if we could just drive by to see if the building was still standing, and it was. He did not go through with it.

I recently remembered a time when I visited him again and he was very drunk. He wanted to leave the apartment where he was visiting, and that meant going down a flight of stairs. He asked me to help him, and half-way down he started to stumble. He was a big man, and his weight could have easily pulled us both down the stairs. Somehow I managed to keep us up there (remember me telling you I was strong then?), and we both survived that too.

When I was already living in Austria and

five months pregnant with my first son, I suddenly had an extremely strong burden to pray for my dad. It was one of only two times in my life I felt a super-strong burden and prayer coming through me, like groaning. I didn't understand why, even though I knew who I was praying for. I knew it was the Holy Spirit interceding through me on my father's behalf. Rom. 8:26 says,

> *"Likewise the Spirit also helps in our weaknesses. For we do not know what we should pray for as we ought, but the Spirit Himself makes intercession for us with groanings which cannot be uttered."*

I had heard nothing from him in over a year, so I had no idea how he was doing nor what was going on in his life at that point in time. But the burden was definitely from the Holy Spirit. I cried, groaned, and interceded for one week. Afterwards I had peace. The day after that my step-mother called to say that my dad had passed away the night before. He was having heart trouble and was in the hospital the last week of his life.

I can only hope that he surrendered his

life to the Lord in that last week. It wasn't until fourteen years later that I got to see where he was buried, on a trip that someone gave us to the United States. That was a very emotional moment for me.

His life and early death proves God's Word that says,

> *"Children, obey your parents in the Lord: for this is right. Honor your father and mother; which is the first commandment with promise;*
> **that it may be well with you, and you may live long on the earth."** *Ephesians 6:1-3*
> (Emphasis mine).

He died just before his 53rd birthday with a lifetime of suffering and pain; I believe it was mainly because he refused to honor or forgive his father.

Sue

My sister's name is Susan, but I always just call her Sue. At eight years of age it became my responsibility to take care of her, since she was only six. For some reason, I hated her when we were growing up. I don't know if it was just my child's mind or my extreme selfishness, or the fact that I always believed that my mother loved her and not me because I looked more like my dad and she looked more like my mom and every time my mom looked at me she was reminded of him. It was probably also due to the fact that it totally overwhelmed me at the time having to be responsible for her. But to my little mind she was to blame and not our parents who put us in those circumstances.

Her life was very difficult as well, and the adult me wishes I could go back and do it over again and care for her better. My mom told her that my dad never wanted her, which I doubt he ever said. But because of the lies (unintentional or not) they caused her a lot of emotional pain, and I did nothing to ease it. In fact, it was probably just the opposite. I caused her even more pain, which hurts my heart very deeply to think about now.

She didn't do too well in school and even ran away from home for a while when she was a little bit older. She started hanging out with the wrong friends who helped her get started smoking and doing drugs at the age of fourteen. She still smokes at the time of this writing (at fifty-eight years of age) and is so desperate to stop.

She moved out of the home sometime after I left, and many years later she also ended up in a relationship where the man had violent tendencies. She went in and out of other abusive relationships after that, as I would have done if the Holy Spirit had not intervened in my life.

After I left for the Air Force we had very little contact. We never wrote and email wasn't a thing in those days, and of course, phone calls were too expensive. I rarely ever called home when she did still live there.

But in spite of all that has happened to her, Sue still has this tenderness about her and is such a caring person. She cares deeply for hurt animals (especially) as well as sick people. She actually has all the qualities of a good, caring nurse. But one of her greatest assets is her ability to retell a story that far exceeds the real thing, be it a book or a movie. That is one of the most amazing things about her, in my opinion. I always think, when she tells me about a movie she has seen, to remind myself not to watch the movie because it will never be as good as her description of it, (I know that from experience) whether it be a comedy or a drama. I keep telling her that she needs to become a writer, because she has such a gift for storytelling.

For more than thirty years, I prayed for my sister's salvation. I visited her when she was fifty-seven years old and she finally gave her heart to Jesus! At the time of this writing, she has not yet been baptized in water nor filled with the Holy Spirit, but that is coming too. I know this is true because I always prayed that she would become a woman of great faith and I am convinced that she will be. And I also believe that the Lord will deliver her from her tobacco habit soon.

Chapter 2 – About God

The First Time I Remember Thinking about God

The first time I even remember thinking about God was after my father left us, when I was eight and my sister was six. My mother was raised Catholic, but she never took us to a Catholic church. She herself, in fact, never went to one at any time I can recall, except right after my dad left. I guess at that time she was desperate to try to find God because she didn't know what to do on her own with two small children so far away from her own family.

We went to a Catholic church, and I distinctly remember her dipping her finger in the water to cross herself (the first time I had ever seen that). She wanted to enter the building but was stopped by a priest. All I remember after that is the three of us standing outside again, and her telling us we were not allowed to go in because she was divorced. Remember, this was fifty-plus years ago. I think the Catholic Church has since changed their policy a bit about letting divorcees into the churches now. Anyway, as we were standing there I remember thinking to myself, *"How could God be so mean to us? At the time when we need Him the most He doesn't let us come in."*

I associated the priest and going to church with God. If you do not know anything about religion nor anything about real Christianity how could you know, especially with a child's mind? One time, I remember asking my mom what the difference was between Catholicism and Christianity. She said they were the same thing. So I grew up thinking everything was the same. That would later become the thinking that that would lead to many years of pain in my life.

My mom never tried to go to any other church or religious group after that experience. As far as I know, that was the end of religion for her too, until she was seventy years old. That was when she finally gave her heart to Jesus and was baptized in a Baptist Church; her salvation happened after more than twenty years of our constant prayer for her and talking to her multiple times about the Lord. She had become very hard over the years and was convinced that she had to do everything in life on her own; that nobody would be there to help her, not even God.

The Navigators

Later, when I was about twelve years of age, my mom sent us to a Church of God where they had a group called the Navigators. In that group children learned about the Bible, Jesus, Salvation, etc. I remember Bible memorization (after I got saved it all came back to me – in the King James Version) and playing games. One time we watched a very scary movie about the Rapture where all the Christians were taken away, and all the other people were left on earth to suffer. I was terrified that I would be left behind (which I think, actually was the name of the movie – *Left Behind*). It was then I started thinking about wanting to get saved, only so that I wouldn't be one of the ones left behind.

The next time we had prayer time they asked us all to bow our heads and then asked us who wanted to ask Jesus into their hearts. I raised my hand but nobody came and led me in a prayer for salvation or even came and talked to me about it. But I firmly believe that Jesus saw my raised hand and was after me from that day on, even though it would take me about eight to nine more years before I surrendered to Him.

Chapter 3 – Military Time
The Military?

My teenage years were very problematic, as is probably the case with most people. My mother, sister and I fought a lot during that time. One day a military recruiter came to the school looking for young people to sign up and become members of the Armed Forces (Military). They came offering testing for glamorous-sounding jobs in the military. If you passed the test you could choose (theoretically) the glamor-job of your choice. Plus they offered things like: world travel, free college education, health benefits and much more. For a girl who was living in poverty with college being a fantasy (but a dream of mine), that seemed impossible. I could never even afford a doctor's visit, so it sounded like the perfect solution. Plus I saw it as my escape to get away from all the fighting at home. Join the military – see the world! Get a free education and free health benefits. Why not?

As I said earlier, my dad used to be a Marine, with the Marines having the reputation of being the toughest of all the branches of the military. The United States also has the Navy,

Army, Air Force and technically the Coast Guard too. Since my dad had been a Marine, after I told him of my idea to enlist in the military, he told me not to join the Army. Marines were not very keen on Army people; they looked down on them – at least at that time. As I arrived at the military recruitment center the first door was the Army, which I obediently skipped over as per Dad's request, and I entered the second door, which was the Air Force.

If the second door I entered had been the Navy, that is where I would have ended up. God really is in control of everything, even when we are not yet living for Him. Later I went to England with the Air Force, which is where I met Reinhard. But the Navy has no bases in England, so I never would have gone there if that second door would have been the Navy. Just imagine when the military was placing different branches in those different offices of that particular building, God made sure that they put the Air Force as the second door. Mind boggling!

With the Air Force, the 'dream-job' I chose was Air Traffic Controller, (the people who work in the control towers to bring the planes in and out of airports safely). We had to take what they called Aptitude Tests to see where our strengths were.

My scores were not good enough for the job I wanted, and I was denied that position. Instead they offered me a job in Air Operations, working with pilots. In reality, at the beginning, it was an office job of filing, etc., that had nothing do to with anything remotely connected to Air Traffic Control. Only much later did I actually get to work with real pilots. But I took the bait anyway and signed up to be in the United States Air Force for four years.

I entered Basic Training (the general training everybody has to go through upon entrance into any military branch) in San Antonio, Texas for six weeks. This is the place where they try to break your will and make you *comply in everything* and follow orders without questioning anything. That is where our own identities ceased to exist, and we all became *GIs*, which stands for *Government Issue*. We no longer belonged to ourselves, we were now property of the United States Government, and they could do with us whatever they wanted. It was there I had my nineteenth birthday.

Supposedly, we could choose where we wanted to be stationed, in which country or State we wanted to serve the military. But even on my list of eight choices, I never entered anywhere near New Mexico, which is where they sent me for four years: in the middle of the dessert! I was a sixteen hour drive from Los Angeles. I know this because I made that drive a number of times in the four years I was stationed there.

But I came to love the dessert. To this day it is one of the favorite places I have ever lived. I saw the beauty in it, where others just saw dry sand, snakes, scorpions and tarantulas. I saw those things too, of course, but thankfully not too often, except the few times I had to flush a scorpion down the drain of my bathtub, or the one time I was at a party and a guy came in with a tarantula on his shoulder. (Shudder!!!)

Another Catholic Priest

My teenage years also got pretty promiscuous, especially once I entered the Air Force. I ended up at one point with a boyfriend who, as I was to find out later in our relationship, could be a bit violent. One time I went off the base where we were all stationed and into the town about twelve miles (about 17.5 km) away. I went with a girlfriend. When I got back he started questioning me about where I had been and with whom and why I didn't tell him I was leaving, which I didn't realize I was supposed to do anyway.

As we stood there talking he started bunching up his fist as if he was getting ready to hit me. Knowing that my father used to beat my mother, I started to get worried that I had picked out the exact same kind of man as well. He never did hit me though. (Later, after we broke up, his next girlfriend and he found out that he had high blood pressure, and he took medication to control it and that was the end of his anger issues.)

But while we were still together, I found

out that I was pregnant by him. When I told him about it he asked me what I was going to do. He never offered to take care of me and the baby, nor did he offer any other kind of help, suggestion or advice.

I remember going to work that day being very depressed and crying. My boss, who was a friend of mine, asked me what was wrong. When I told him, he became very disgusted with me, because in those days (the end of the 1970's) a pregnancy was a bad thing to have *happen* to you. And that was the end of our friendship. But his advice to me was to go to the base chapel, which is like a multi-national church with many different denominations represented.

When I entered the chapel the lady at the front desk asked me what denomination I was. Since I wasn't a Christian at the time I replied, *"Any, they are all the same"*. Remember, I got that from my mom. She went to see who was available and sent me a Catholic priest.

When I explained my situation to him he asked me, *"Is the father going to marry you?"* to which I replied, *"It doesn't look like it."* Then he said, *"Can you take care of a child on your own?"* and I said, *"I don't see how"*. Then he said, *"Then there is no choice, you have to get an abortion."* I was totally shocked! That was not even a thought in my mind. But I tried to argue and say that there must be some other way. Then he got angry with me and was practically yelling at me, *"If he is not going to marry you, and you can't take care of the baby on your own, you have no choice!"* And in my mind I was thinking that God was telling me that I had to do this thing.

I found a military doctor, because civilian doctors who did abortions were rare in those days. He also treated me with disgust, because abortions were something very uncommon, and anyone who had one carried great disgrace and humiliation with them afterwards. The doctor did a bad job and in the end had not removed the entire baby. I had to go to the hospital some time later to have things repaired.

After leaving the doctor's office, on the way home I saw a billboard on the side of the road that said, *"Abortion is murder."* That was the start of three years of deep guilt and condemnation.

Prior to learning I was pregnant I was having some dental work done. In those days, they didn't automatically put the big, heavy lead barrier across women to protect them from the radiation. When the technician asked me if I was pregnant I, of course, answered no because I didn't know that I was. Even if I would have gone through with the birth of the baby, it would have been very deformed or had some kind of major disabilities due to the radiation that it had received at that time in its development, which must have been only a few weeks, at the most.

When I met my boyfriend again after everything had been *taken care of,* he acted like everything was back to normal, and we could carry on as we did before the *mishap.* But I couldn't handle being with someone who seemed so insensitive and uncaring, so I broke off the relationship. He cried very much, which hurt me, but not enough to change my mind about ending the relationship.

The Next Relationship

Many months later I started another relationship with a man who was caring and a good talker and listener, which at that time was very important to me. My ex-boyfriend had trouble talking about anything personal in his life, but my new one did it with such ease. In fact, I had never met a man before who could communicate so openly and freely about so many things, even personal things, which created a desire in me to want to marry him. Communication is important to a woman, after all.

This boyfriend had some friends who did different kinds of drugs. As a teenager, before entering the military, whenever drugs entered a room I was in, I would leave by a different exit. I didn't want anything to do with them. But my new boyfriend had somehow convinced me to try marijuana. We ended up going to lots of parties with alcohol and all kinds of drugs, although I just stuck to the marijuana, except two times. A pilot, I used to babysit for, argued with me for an hour each time to try cocaine. Those were the only two times I ever did, and I did not want to then or ever again.

One day my boyfriend and I had been out somewhere, and we came home and got ready to go to another party, where I knew drugs would be again. I reckoned in my heart that marijuana couldn't be that bad because it was a plant, and God had made the plants, which is a typical thing many druggies say to validate their use of it.

We were living in military housing, barracks, as they were called. This is like a big building with a bunch of single rooms connected by one bathroom between two rooms. We both lived in the same barracks of the many on the base. Anyway, as we were entering the building I prayed, *"God, if it is not right to go to this party then please give me a sign."* We went in and showered and returned within about 15-20 minutes. When we got back in the car again he tried to start it but it wouldn't start. We found out that the alternator was dead, not just the battery. I really felt that God was saying to me that it was not right to do any kind of drugs.

Somehow we got to the party anyway,

but I think I tried to stay away from all drugs – that day at least. At the party, even though it was loud and very noisy, they had the TV on. I don't think the sound was turned up but I happened to glance at it, and a Jesus movie was playing. I don't think the people who were hosting the party were even aware of what was on. But I was mesmerized by what I saw. It was the part where Jesus had the cross on his back and was being led to the crucifixion. I couldn't take my eyes off the screen. It affected me so deeply that I was wondering if other people were seeing it too. I tried to get some people's attention to show them this deep, moving experience at that moment on TV. Nobody paid any attention. I think I even started crying. God was reaching out to me again, and an awareness of him started awakening within me.

My boyfriend had always just said that he was an agnostic; he didn't really care one way or the other about such things. After we had been together for about a year, I felt very strongly that I really wanted to marry him. By this time I had started reading my Bible more and tried to pray, as best I could. One day I prayed, *"Lord, I really want to marry this man. But I also want to do your will. So please give me a sign."* Two weeks later my military unit (called a squadron in the Air Force) had to go for two weeks to do some special training in Florida. Since I was working with the pilots of fighter jets at that time, I had to go too.

While there I had a day off work and a colleague asked me if I wanted to go to Disney World, which was a four hour drive away. But we were young and had energy so I agreed. On the way back I saw a sign in front of a church. I like the way the churches in the States always put up these cute little statements in front of them to make you think, and I always like to read them. This sign said, *"It is worth it to wait for God's very best for you."* And I knew, that I knew, that I knew that God had spoken to me.

My first reaction was obviously loud as I said, *"That was a real sign."* The guy next to me said, *"What did you say?"* My next thought was, *"I can't tell him that Almighty God just spoke to me! Who am I that God would speak to me?"* But I was still sure that he just did. I said to the friend, *"Nothing."* But kept thinking about this for about half an hour, and then said to God, *"Ok, God, then I will settle for second best"*, because I had already settled in my heart that I wanted to marry my boyfriend. Isn't that just so human? We ask God what he wants for us and then try to go ahead and do what we want anyway.

My Appendix

When I was 21 years old I decided to drive home on Saturday for Easter weekend to visit my mom and sister. The day after I got there (Easter Sunday) I got really sick. I was in bed with lots of pain, high fever and vomiting. My mom just said, *"Oh, it is the stomach flu. It's going around right now."* But she wouldn't take me to see a doctor. The pain in my lower abdomen got so bad that I couldn't even make it to the bathroom on my own; she had to come and walk me there and back.

On Tuesday my dad had found out that I was in town and happened to call me. I asked him if he had a car, and if he would take me to the hospital to get something checked out. He came immediately. We went to one hospital first for veterans, and they sent us to a Navy hospital since I was active duty, or still in the military, as opposed to being a veteran, already finished with my time in the armed services. I was admitted immediately, and the doctor couldn't figure out what the problem was, so said he would do exploratory surgery the next day.

Both my mom and dad were there together with me in the hospital, and even though it had been thirteen years since he had left our family, when I saw them together I said, *"It is nice to see you two together again."* I guess the little kid inside us always wants our parents to be together, like it should be.

In the meantime, my squadron back in New Mexico had issued an AWOL report for me which means, *Absent Without Leave*. That meant that if I would have happened to have been pulled over by a policeman, and he ran my driver's license through his computer, he would have found out that I was a fugitive, and he would have arrested me on the spot. That all got sorted out after I got back and explained to them that I was in the hospital the whole time and was not trying to run away from the Air Force.

But back to the hospital… The doctor told my parents that the surgery would last about forty-five minutes. After well over two hours later the doctors came out and said that my appendix had ruptured, but that something called an abscess had formed inside my abdomen (or something like that) and caught all the poisons from it, which is why it didn't kill me. Apparently it had ruptured two days before I went to the hospital and three days before the surgery. It was a total miracle that I was still alive! God was watching out for me even though I was still not surrendered to Him yet.

I ended up staying in the hospital for two weeks because when they cut open your stomach apparently your whole digestion system stops, and they don't let you leave again until it starts. Mine hadn't started yet, and after the two weeks the doctor came into my room and said that the next day he would have to go in again to see what was wrong. Up until that point I couldn't even have a sip of water. They said it would rot in my stomach. Yuck. That evening I prayed, *"God, if you let my system start I will live for you,"* you know, one of *those kinds* of prayers. That very night my system started again. But I didn't associate it with my prayer or God, until about two years later.

Not too long afterwards my boyfriend started stealing from the Air Force and eventually got caught, put into prison, discharged out of the

Air Force and sent back home to New Hampshire, where he was from. This is on the opposite coast from California, where I was from, and where they would send me back when my time was finished, in about one more year.

But my life kept getting worse and worse, along with my reputation. Then one day, suddenly the Air Force offered me a *special duty assignment* in England working for the Post Office on the military base there. I was really torn because one of the places I wanted to see when I joined the military was England. On the other hand I wanted to get out of the Air Force. I called my boyfriend to ask what he thought I should do and was expecting him to say that I should come to him, and we would get married. But instead he was just trying to be nice and said, *"You should do what you want to do"*, which angered me because he didn't speak out his love for me. In anger I signed the papers.

After a few days I was much calmer and then regretted my decision and tried to get out of it. But they wouldn't let me. I tried to get my commander to get me out of it but he couldn't either. In the military once you sign something it might as well be in blood – it is permanent! Then I thought, *"Maybe this is God trying to get me out of all this mess here."*

I didn't just have bad experiences in the Air Force though. One great thing that happened to me, that a rare few people *ever* get to experience, is that I got to fly for one hour in an F-15 Eagle fighter jet. That is an experience of a lifetime! (That is the picture of me having just returned from my flight, on the back cover). I borrowed a suit from one of the pilots and one of my personal friends flew the plane. We did an exercise with the base General. (Pilots have to practice all different kinds of exercises, maneuvers and drills to be ready for anything). We had to try to 'shoot' each other down. The only problem with that was that our radar went out just after we finished our 90 degree take-off, that's right – straight up! We were both looking everywhere when suddenly I saw the General at our 6 o'clock (that's pilot talk for *directly behind us*). I yelled but it was too late as we heard the words over our radio, *"Guns, guns, guns,"* which meant that he just shot us down.

I also flew in many other types of aircraft, including an air-to-air refueler. I got some great pictures of us refueling an F-16 fighter jet in mid-air. I was also in a number of different helicopters (including a Black Hawk) and once we flew through a ravine so fast I was just hoping the pilot was as good as he thought he was. One time I got to fly in a helicopter in Florida, and we were shown a sunken ship that was clearly visible from the air. It was really cool. I was also in some transport or cargo planes (sometimes for a free trip back to see my mom), from England.

The

New

Me

Chapter 4 – Finding God
The Plane Ride to England and Getting Saved

When I finally boarded the plane heading to England it was with some mixed feelings. I didn't know anybody over there. Since that was the case I prayed, *"Lord, I don't know anybody in England, so I will live for you completely."*

The very first person I met on my new base immediately offered me drugs. I refused, determined to start living for God now. The next person I met was another Air Force girl on the base who invited me to go to the base chapel with her. With my experience from the last time I went to a base chapel in mind, and the fact that I thought that I could be a Christian alone, without having to go to a boring church, I politely declined her invitation.

The next two weeks my life took a downward spiral and I ended up in a hotel room with a pilot I had just met. It was then I realized that I didn't have what it took to be a Christian. The very next day that same girl came to me and asked me again if I wanted to go to the chapel with her. I reluctantly agreed thinking that now my life was over. I would have a boring Christian life in a boring church. I went with her, and it was as boring as I expected.

Then she said that some of the airmen (as we were called in the Air Force), were going to meet together that night for a Bible study and asked if I wanted to go. To be truthful I did not want to, but to be polite I went with her, and to my surprise I met true, born-again Christians there who were having a great time and really enjoying the Lord. I went regularly after that.

One time she invited me to go with some people from the group to this church off the base, (a civilian church, ohhh) and I was in for a surprise. When we got there the worship had already started, and I just stood there in shock. There were people raising their hands and singing, and there were guitars and even drums…in a church! I had only ever seen churches with an organ, or a modern one perhaps with a piano, but never anything like this before. I really liked it.

Later we found a very small Assembly of

God church very close to our base, and some of us started to go there. They were waiting to get a new pastor at the time, and I was learning about stuff like Baptism and wanted it now! But they said the new pastor would baptize me when he came in a few months. Thus began the long wait.

Assembly Days

At some point before the new pastor had arrived I was born again, unlike most people I cannot clearly tell you the exact date and time. In my opinion it was on the plane when I told Him I would live for Him from that point on. I clearly remember the day the new pastor finally did arrive though. As we were all introducing ourselves I immediately said, *"Can you baptize me?"* He was very polite and just asked me to hold on a few more days until they could organize a baptism. The day I finally came up out of that water was amazing! I had been waiting for it for months and the feeling of freedom I experienced was wonderful.

I went to him for counseling very soon after his arrival and confessed the abortion. I told him that I knew that God had forgiven me for what I had done, but even after having been a Christian for a while I was still plagued by guilt and couldn't get rid of it. He told me that I needed to forgive that Catholic Priest for what he told me to do. I had never even thought of that. I forgave him and felt immediate peace, which has lasted until this day.

Our pastor was, in fact, an amazing Bible teacher. I got such a strong foundation being under his teachings, that I believe it gave me a head-start in my Christian walk with God. He started teaching us about the baptism in the Holy Spirit, and I had never heard of that before. But I felt that anything God had for me I wanted. After the service he invited those who wanted to be baptized in the Holy Spirit to come to the front. Basically the whole church did, we were only about twenty or thirty people at that time. As far as I can remember, everybody received the baptism except me and one other man. Everyone started speaking in tongues, as is the evidence of the baptism in the Holy Spirit. Acts 10:44-46 is just one scripture,

> *"While Peter was still speaking these words, the Holy Spirit fell upon all those who heard the word. And those of the circumcision who believed were astonished, as many as came with Peter, because the gift of the Holy Spirit had been poured out on the Gentiles also. **For they heard them speak with tongues** and magnify God."* (My emphasis).

I went home totally frustrated thinking that something was wrong with me. It was at that time I clearly heard the voice of God speak to me. He said, *"I want you to go and ask that young man that you said bad things about, to forgive you."* Just the week prior to that I had stood up in the mess hall (military dining area) and said something very loudly about a man who had just previously said something, and I had humiliated him by my words. Now, being the extremely proud person that I was, I was very reluctant to do what God had just said that I should do.

You know sometimes when God tells you to do something then doesn't let you off the hook until you do it? Well, a few days later I was riding the bus, which happened to make a particular stop, which is where I got out. The only other person who also got out at that stop was the man God had told me to ask for forgiveness, and he was walking in the exact same direction as I was going. I kind of just said to God, *"Ok, ok. I'll do it!"* Then I walked over to the young man and told him I was sorry for the things I had said about him the previous week. He said that it was fine, and I thought that everything was sufficient then.

The next weekend I went forward again for the baptism in the Holy Spirit and again, nothing happened. This time I was really frustrated because I thought that I was obedient, and I still didn't get what I was expecting from God. On the way home this time the Lord said, *"I didn't tell you to say 'I'm sorry' I told you to ask him to forgive you."* I tried to argue that they were the same thing, but guess who wins when you argue with God?

About another week went by, and one day I found myself just happening to be walking past his room in the barracks, and I finally gave in. I knocked on the door, and when I entered he was very shocked to see me there. This time I apologized for my bad behavior *and* asked him to forgive me. He said, *"I forgive you. Can we forget about this now?"* I said, *"**Now** we can."* And I went to my room knowing I had finally been obedient to God.

I felt so good inside. I started reading my Bible, and I happened to read a parable of Jesus. I felt frustrated because I did not understand it. I put my Bible away and did what I normally never did; I started to pray out loud. I said,

"Lord, I really need your Holy Spirit to come and help me understand what I am reading here" (not at all meaning the baptism at this point). And as I continued to pray, suddenly I no longer understood the words coming out of my mouth. I remember them sounding Chinese to me. I gasped and then grabbed my Bible again and opened it to the same parable and read it. This time I understood everything written! I closed my Bible again and laid on my bed and spoke in tongues until I went to sleep.

One time the base needed our barracks (remember, those are the living quarters of the military men and women) to house more men. There were only about three to four of us women on one-half of a floor of a whole two-story building. The base commander had decided that he would just put us women on the top floor of one of the men's barracks and use ours for other men. But according to base regulations, that wasn't allowed, mainly for the safety of the women. One of my friends had already received rape threats. As I was praying about it, I felt strongly that God did not want this to happen, and He told me to go and tell the base commander.

Now, let us just imagine this for a moment. One of the lowest ranking people on the base (me) was told by God to go and tell the base commander (the highest ranking person on base) that God did not want those women to move in there. So what did I do? I argued with God, of course. Then I actually went to the base commander and told him what God had said. At first he looked at me like I was crazy or something. Throughout the conversation he was very kind, maybe because he saw how much I was shaking. And then he dismissed me.

The whole plan was delayed for a few months or so until the commander could try to figure something else out. In the end, they decided to add safety doors to the women's area so the men couldn't have free access, and then they moved the women over there anyway, because they were just so desperate for the rooms. But I, instead, moved into what is called base housing with a family, who I already knew, the wife of who became my very best friend. I lived with them for nine months.

I had many experiences during those nine months that I lived there. During that time I remember praying some strange prayers. Prayers like, *"God, I don't like things the way they are, but I don't want You to change anything - I'm not leaving you much room to work, am I?"* and *"Oh, Lord, I want to be on the front lines of the battle for you."* Of course, I had no idea at the time what *'front lines of the battle'* meant.

I had to share a bed with their teenage daughter but she was away at school during the week and only home on the weekends. It was also during that time that I had my recurring problems with my menstruation, being extremely heavy and extending many days. It got to the point where I had to use tampons, plus pads and get up two or three times a night to change everything just to keep the bed from being ruined. Then it got worse and I used black, plastic trash bags to tie around myself before going to bed at night which I took off in the bathtub in the morning. I would usually have to end up throwing away another pair of underwear.

When I finally asked God to heal me I clearly heard God say, *"Then leave off the trash bag.*" I was terrified, firstly because it was not my bed and secondly because I have to admit, my faith was not all that strong at that point. I waited a few more months, and then I finally agreed to God's will. I went to bed one night without the bag. I had to get up only one time in the night to change one pad, and by the morning everything was fine.

Chapter 5 – A Defining Moment
Decision Time

Soon it was going to be time for me to get out of the Air Force and go back to the States. A few months prior to my exit date, the Air Force came to me and asked me what I intended to do: extend my enlistment for another four years or get out and return to California. As I was praying about it, I felt the Lord had said to me that He wanted me to get out and go back to California to a Christian college. I said, *"Lord, I believe that this is what you are telling me to do. If I am wrong, please tell me clearly."*

About two weeks before I was supposed to separate (what getting out of the military is called), I was in a meeting and my pastor was preaching about the life of Abraham. He started by saying that God had called him out of his own land. And I was thinking, *"Me too."* Then God sent him to a land he had never been to before. I said, *"Me too."* And this about Abraham's life and that about his life, and after every point I was saying, *"Me too."* Then finally he finished talking about Abraham's past and started talking about his future and he said, seemingly forcefully, *"And God told him to remain in the land where he now was."* It hit me so loud and clear. God was telling me to get out of the Air Force and to stay in England!

The next day I ran to the office on base and told them that I was still separating but that the paperwork needed to be changed because I was staying in England. Somehow it all worked out and there I was, stranded in England with nowhere to go and no means of support, because the condition of my visa was that I was not allowed to work. My pastor and his wife let me live with them, and I passed the time by cleaning their house, and a few houses of neighbors and some people from the church. The people weren't allowed to pay me but occasionally they were allowed to give me a few pounds (British money).

After many months of waiting for what God wanted me to do next, one day my pastor comes to me and says, *"I think you should go to IBTI."* That was the Bible school he had attended about five years previously. It was called the International Bible Training Institute and was an Assembly of God Bible school founded and run purely on faith. They had students literally from all over the world who were foreign nationals trained and then sent back to their own countries because they already understood the language, the culture, etc.

But in those days you only went to Bible school if you were going to be a missionary in Africa, at least, that's what I thought. I said to my pastor, *"If God wants me to go there then He can tell me."* To which he replied, *"Maybe He just did, through me."* And my answer was something that he himself had taught us, *"Then He can confirm it."* He always told us that we don't base our future plans on what somebody else says we should do but wait for God to tell us personally His will for us.

The very next day I was doing my regular Bible reading and I *happened* to read Hebrews 13:7 which says,

> *"Remember those who rule over you, who have spoken the word of God to you, whose faith follow, considering the outcome of their conduct."*

So I said, *"Looks like I'm going to IBTI."* I applied for entrance for the very next semester knowing that I would be accepted because God told me to go, even though they could have only chosen about fifty students of all the hundreds of applications they receive each year. But they prayed over every single one they received and mine was accepted (no surprise to me).

Chapter 6 – Training, In More Ways Than One
I.B.T.I. Days

One of the first things that happened at IBTI was that this little Austrian dude came up to me the very first week and announced to me that he was going to marry me. I told him very clearly that he was not! But he was persistent. Just about a week prior to him approaching me I had read in Isaiah 54:5 where it says,

> *"**For your Maker is your husband**, the Lord of hosts is His name; and your Redeemer is the Holy One of Israel; He is called the God of the whole earth."* (Emphasis mine).

I was absolutely convinced at that point that I would never get married, because God was my husband. I had even asked Him for strength to remain single for Him forever, and I meant it with my whole heart.

After Reinhard had started talking to me so much about marrying me, God started talking to me about it too, and I was very confused. Finally He gave me a Bible verse to confirm it, and within the week I had seen, received or *accidentally* saw that exact same verse seven times. Finally I gave in and agreed to start hanging out with Reinhard. I don't really want to say which verse it was here because it would make no sense to anyone except me.

Not too long before I had exited the military I was heavily into bodybuilding. When I say heavily into, I mean, like four to six hours a day six days a week. I was very strong! Then in my church I was put in charge of forming a youth group, since we didn't have one. A friend and I went to town, and I challenged some of the young boys to come to our church for an arm-wrestling competition against me. We told them that if I won they had to stay and listen to what we had to say. If they were to win, we had promised them something. I can't remember what now. They came, I won and they listened. Unfortunately, they didn't return, and we never really got a youth group going.

But my pastor thought it was funny. The semester before I went to IBTI my pastor had gone there to help them with something. While he was there he told the students who would be there the next semester that he had a lady who would be coming who was the arm-wrestling champion of America. I was so embarrassed when he told me that. Apparently, immediately after my pastor had said that about me God had spoken to Reinhard, and told him that I would be his wife. Basically the minute I arrived, Reinhard was one of the first people who took me by the arm and sat me down at a table to arm wrestle. He put his brother, who was a carpenter, across from me and locked our hands together to do arm-wrestling. I immediately pulled away and told them that was my old life, and I don't do that anymore. What else could I have said?

Apparently, I had also started a rumor at that time that I had a tattoo as well. At one point, for some reason, I had to go away from the Bible school for a few hours a week. I don't remember the real reason, but some of the girls were asking what I was doing, and I just told them that I was going to get a tattoo removed. I believe that on our wedding night Reinhard was secretly looking for the tattoo that he still believed I had somewhere on my body. Those were the days when ladies didn't have a tattoo.

One day I was at a church in another town in England, and while I was there I heard very clearly that God was going to restore my virginity. I was overwhelmed and started to cry.

It seemed almost too good to be true, but I knew that nothing was impossible for God, so I humbly accepted the gift. If we would have lived in the age of modern cell phones and selfies and always having cameras available, I would have taken a picture on my wedding night of the blood on the sheet as proof of God's promise to me being fulfilled.

I learned a number of lessons at IBTI and also experienced some strange things while I was there. One of the first lessons I learned was from an incident that happened during our kitchen duty one morning. All the students had to help do chores or duties throughout the day and this particular morning I was in charge of getting breakfast ready for the students and staff. There was a group assigned to help me, one of whom was a young Italian man. I told him to do something, and he got so offended at me because, *"A woman does not tell a man what to do!"*

I was under time pressure and not so patient and loving at that moment, and told him I don't care what he believes he has to go and get the stuff ready that I told him to do. He didn't speak to me for days afterwards, which didn't really bother me, until one day the Lord told me to go and ask him for forgiveness. I started to argue that he was the one at fault, and why should I have to go and ask him to forgive me? The Lord told me that it was because I was responsible for my brother's heart, and his was not doing well at that moment. The forgiveness was not for me but for him. I did as I was told and the relationship was restored as well as his heart's attitude.

Another incident occurred because the Air Force had found out later that when they had hurried the separation papers, they had made a financial mistake in my favor, and now they wanted their money back. I was by now in my second year at Bible school, and when I returned the money to them it now meant that I was penniless (apparently exactly where the Lord needed me to be to learn some new lessons in faith).

The first lesson came after I had gone to town many months earlier to pick out a wedding dress because Reinhard and I had gotten engaged (explained later). I didn't have the money to buy it right away but they had a special arrangement where someone could leave some money at the shop, and they would keep the merchandise in the shop until it was paid off in monthly installments. I guess it was like America's lay-away plans. I only had to pay about 5 pounds a month, and I was in no hurry to pick it up because I still had at least a year before we were planning on getting married.

Many months later, I was praying and telling the Lord that I needed some paper and pencils or something, and I told the Lord that I was two months behind on my payments for the wedding dress. I told him that I was in the exact right place that He wanted me to be, so I needed His help financially that day.

I went downstairs, and I saw that there was an envelope in my mailbox, although the mail hadn't come yet that day. I took the envelope, went upstairs to try to find a quiet place and opened it and read,

"My God shall supply all your need according to His riches in glory by Christ Jesus." (Phil 4:19)

It wasn't signed, and there was a 100 pound note inside. I started crying. I thought, *"Lord, I knew you loved me, but I didn't know it was that much."* I went to town to buy all the materials I needed, and I could take the wedding dress home from the shop that very day. God had given me enough money to pay it off completely!

Another incident happened one day when I was again out of money. But this time I knew that God would provide for me. I needed some things for my menstruation days and asked the Lord for His provision or for the bleeding to stop. I was fine with either way. I went to the chapel to pray and afterwards a lady came up to me and whispered, *"Debi, there is blood on the back of your skirt."* I was devastated. It seemed like God had let me down.

When classes started I was still in my room crying. When the director's husband asked where I was the students told him. He came to check on me thinking I was sick. When he asked me what was wrong I said that I couldn't talk to him about it. He asked me if I would talk to his wife, the director of the school. I said I would. When I told her the story she apologized to me, and said that it was her fault. I didn't understand.

She explained to me that the school at the bottom of our driveway used to be a private school for boys and girls. They were switching over to an all-boys school, and the director of that school came over to our director (her) with a whole box of things for girls' monthly periods, pads, etc. But since she was such a 'proper British woman' she was disgusted that he had even asked her such a question and refused to take them. Because of her pride, my answer was delayed. I say delayed because she took me to town and bought me everything I needed that day.

God never lets us down, but that day I found out that we could be the blockage to other people's prayers being answered.

Self-Moving Legs

Two times at the school something very strange happened to me. Both times it was as though God Himself (or probably an angel) actually took control of my legs and moved them against my will.

The first time was after a lecture from a pastor of a big church in the north of England. He had preached about knowing the love of God. Then he said that he would be available to anyone afterward who wanted to talk to him about that subject or any other. After the class I was on *kitchen duty* and had to run to get the tables set for lunch. Halfway to the kitchen my legs turned around and started walking back to the classroom, and I had no control what-so-ever. I ended up standing right in front of him and felt totally stupid because I had no idea why, or even how, I was there. To ease my embarrassment somewhat I said, *"Uh, I think I have to talk to you later."* He said ok and then we marked a time after lunch.

When I got to the meeting I told him that I had no idea why I was there. He kind of laughed and said that it was ok, and that we would just talk. I ended up leaving that appointment with the deepest sense of the love of God for me that I had ever felt. For weeks afterwards every time someone would ask how I was I would respond with, *"Loved by God."*

The second time it happened I had just previously talked to one of the Italian girls about her problems with menstruation. She would have such bad cramps and pain that she was usually in bed for about a week. I told her God would heal her because He healed me. But I didn't force anything on her and just went to the chapel meeting, which was mandatory for all the students.

After the meeting I noticed that she was at the back of the room by the back door, on her knees praying with her head in her hands on the chair. I was thinking about going over to pray for her but I didn't want to push her. I decided to just leave the meeting and get ready for bed. I put my hand on the doorknob to open the back door and my right leg went up and over her so that now she was underneath me. I had no control over that movement; it happened without my permission or will.

Since I was straddling her, and it felt uncomfortable, I quickly picked up my other leg and put it on the other side as well, so that now I was standing on the other side of her. Again, being embarrassed and not knowing what to say or do, I bent down and asked her if she wanted me to pray for her. She mumbled that she did without ever looking up. I prayed and quickly left the room. Later that night she told me that she wasn't sure if the Lord wanted to heal her or not, but if it was His will then she asked Him to send me over to her to pray for her. Wow! She was much better in the following months.

Reinhard and I had gotten engaged during my first and his second year at Bible school at midnight between the eighth and ninth of August, because his birthday is the eight and mine is the ninth. So romantic! Well, sort of romantic. We broke about three rules or more that night to do so. First of all, we were supposed to be in bed by a certain time and asleep. Secondly, boys and girls (men and women) weren't allowed to be alone together.

Thirdly, no alcohol was allowed on the premises of the school.

Just after midnight, (having sneaked out of bed still fully clothed) we were in the garden shed on a blanket by candlelight celebrating with a glass of sweet white wine. Suddenly the door opened, and the man in charge of the students stood in front of us and just stared at us for a moment before saying, *"I want to see how you explain this to the director in the morning."* He then shut the door and left.

We thought that we were already in trouble so we might as well finish celebrating. In the morning Reinhard thought that he would beat the man to the director and confess everything. The director was actually not surprised and even said that the leadership team already thought that we should be together but that we should just keep away from each other and keep it quiet. We did that and everything was fine.

During my second year Reinhard was working at a church about a few hours' drive away. We telephoned occasionally. During one of those calls something happened and during a very big misunderstanding we broke off the engagement. Reinhard was actually devastated, but I suddenly had peace, which I thought was strange because I was sure that God wanted me to marry him. After Bible school I ended up going back to the States and was there for about a year. Neither of us heard one word from each other during that time, as he went back to Austria.

Chapter 7 – Here, There and Everywhere
Unsettled

After having been back in the States for about a year, I was feeling like such a foreigner in my own country, that I decided to go back to England. I thought that I would just go and visit the Bible school secretary, since she and I were good friends, and then go and stay with my pastor and his wife for a while. Little did I know that once you left the country the visa then became null and void. I arrived in England, and when they were processing me, the lady said that I didn't have a visa to come in and told me mine was no good.

Then she asked me how much money I had, and it was very little. She said, *"You don't even have enough money to buy a ticket home if I don't let you in!"* I told her I would call my dad for the money. When she asked what he did, I couldn't tell her he worked in a bar. I just said, *"Well, I can call my mom."* After enquiring about what my mom did, which was that she was unemployed, I thought and then said, *"I will get the money somewhere."* In reality I had no backup plan and no way to get any money. She just told me to go and wait until she had finished processing the plane, and in the meantime another plane came in from Australia. I sat there for over two hours. While I was waiting I prayed, *"Lord, I thought you told me to come back here. If not then you have to tell me where you want me to go and help me get there. I trust you."* I waited in total peace.

After she called me to talk to her, she asked me a lot of questions, *"What will you do? Where will you live?"* And a bunch more I can't even remember right now. My answers were very unsure. I just said, *"Well, maybe I can do this. Maybe I can stay with my pastor and his wife, etc."* She asked for my pastor's phone number to call him.

Now I thought he would be mad because I didn't even tell him I was coming, and he had a small problem with impatience. She called him, and she told me later that he had basically said everything exactly as I had said to her with all the maybe's etc. She then said she would have to talk to her supervisor. When she came back, she said that her supervisor said it was ok. Then she asked me how long I wanted the visa for. Up until that point I had had one for four months or six months, not counting the time I was studying. I thought for a second and then said, *"For one year?"* She looked at me for a minute like I was crazy and then she just said, *"OK"*, and stamped my visa for one year.

On Again

At some point during the year that I had returned to England, Reinhard and I had *accidentally* met up again at IBTI. This time we knew that we were supposed to get married, but that the timing wasn't right. We had tried to rush it the first time. We were learning about God's proper timing for everything. We were now officially engaged again, but still planned to go our separate ways until the time was right. I am convinced (now) that the misunderstanding that led to the break-up was because we were trying to rush God's will for our lives. The timing of God is more important than we really realize.

I ended up back in the States after some time in England, and Reinhard went back to Austria. We wrote letters to each other trying to find a date to arrange the wedding, which was to take place in Austria. After many weeks of letter writing, Reinhard finally decided it was enough. He decided to call even though a one minute phone call was like $4 then, in the 1980's. We kept it brief (about ten minutes) and settled on a date, 25 October 1986. He said to me, *"You believe God to get you here, and I will believe God for a Honeymoon."* But I was unemployed and needed a job. I asked him to pray with me for a job. He asked me what job I wanted, and after a few minutes thought, I said that I wanted a delivery job with UPS, which is one of the biggest package delivery services in the States, (or at least it was at that time).

Mc D's and a Puppy

My mom and my step-father (she married again about sixteen years after her divorce) were living in northern California at that time. I moved in with them and temporarily got a job at the McDonald's in their town. I went to a small church in the town. I started evangelizing a boy who worked at McDonald's with me who was homeless and from New York.

He was nineteen now but his mother threw him out he was about sixteen, when she got a new boyfriend. He traveled all the way across the country and ended up in California where he had gotten a girl under eighteen pregnant and went to jail because of that for a bit. He lived in a tent in the woods and had a tiny puppy, which he tied up outside the McDonald's while he was at work.

One day we came out of work, and someone had stolen his puppy. He was devastated. To the homeless, animals are usually the only family they have. I told him I would pray for God to send it back, and the next day it was there again, tied up just where he had left it. His heart opened a little bit for God.

One day he asked me to take him somewhere to see his parole officer, but he had lied to me. We ended up meeting his girlfriend, the one he had gotten pregnant, who he was not allowed to see. But on the way, as we were walking, I prayed out loud that the Lord would help us *find some food* for the dog. Then the dog literally found a bowl of puppy or kitten food under a bush.

The young man was so shocked because it happened exactly as I had prayed. Then I asked him to go to church with me, and he did. I had been telling him so many things, and when the preaching started the pastor was saying some of the exact same words that I had said to him. He looked at me again with a shocked look on his face. I told him that was God speaking to him. He didn't get saved while I was there, but he got a good bit closer to the Lord, that is for sure.

God's Faithfulness, a Witness to My Relatives, and an Angel

I ended up driving cross country with my mom and step-father to the new place in Georgia where they were moving at the time. Then I went up to Pennsylvania to live with some of my relatives. I ended up in the house of my paternal grandmother's sister, or in other words, my great-aunt. I needed to find a job, so I walked up one side of her town and down the other and went into every shop asking people if they were hiring. Nobody was.

After I was on my way back and feeling very discouraged, I wasn't paying much attention where I was going and nearly walked into a man who crossed my path. It was a UPS delivery driver. Then God said to me, *"You asked for a job with UPS. Aren't you even going to see if you can get one with them?"* I had totally forgotten all about it. I waited for the driver to come out of the shop and asked him about getting a job with them, where and how, etc. He told me that the company was, in fact, hiring at the moment and gave me the address. I went to the address and filled out the application. It just so happened that year that the government was putting requirements on companies to hire more women and veterans, and I was both. The company had no choice but to hire me, over the three or five other men who applied that day.

Since that was only a part-time job, I needed to look for another one. I ended up getting a job in a tiny 7/11 store where I was the night shift, because they were opened twenty-four hours a day. I had to clean, replenish stock and serve any customers who came in. The only problem was that this store was very secluded, out in the woods practically, where it was dark and lonely.

But I wasn't afraid, except one night. A car of young people, two boys and a girl, drove into the parking lot and pulled into the parking space next to the door, backwards (as if to make a quick get-away). I immediately sensed that I was about to get robbed. I quickly called the police, who in the end took twenty minutes to get there! The young people stayed outside as long as I had customers. One time they did come in, and the girl looked really mean. They bought something then went and sat in the car, waiting.

When the police finally did arrive, I told them I thought I was about to get robbed. They looked over to the magazine area by the front window and said to me, *"By that guy?"* I looked up and saw a man with long hair and an army jacket who had his back to me. I never saw him come in, he never bought anything and I never saw his face, nor did I see when he left. I told the police no, that I thought it was the kids in the car outside. They asked me if I had written down the license number, but in my nervousness I had never even thought about it. Finally everybody left (except that man I just told you about that I never saw leave, but he wasn't there anymore) and things went on as normal. I never had another threat. Later I thought that God had sent his angel to protect me.

But there was another problem. I was working in the store at least five days a week, and sometimes UPS would call me and ask me to work the next day, which was usually a ten-hour shift. That meant that sometimes I worked eighteen to twenty-three hours a day a few days a week. That took a toll on my body, and I ended up with a spinal infection and anemia. I slept for one week straight, day and night. Finally my grandmother said she would pay for me to go to a doctor. I went, and that's how I found out what I had. Then I determined that I would go back to a church that my other Aunt had taken me to once, and I would ask the pastor to anoint me with oil and pray for me. And I knew that I would be healed.

I went to the meeting and handed the pastor a piece of paper stating my request. Then during worship the leader said that we don't need the pastor to pray for us because we can pray for each other to be healed, or for whatever else we needed. The lady behind me tapped me on the shoulder and asked me if I was in pain, to which I replied that I was. She said she could tell. She told me that God used her in healing even though she was very sick herself. I think she said that she had cancer or something that serious.

She prayed for me, and we both felt a heat wave surge through our bodies. I was instantly healed. Then the pastor got up and announced to the church that the Holy Spirit had woken him up the night before to pray, because the next day he was going to anoint the sick, and they would be healed. He told them that this young lady whom he had never met before (and asked me if that was true, and I was nodding my head furiously in agreement) came and handed him a paper requesting anointing with oil for healing. He asked me to come forward.

I asked him if I could say something first. I told him I wrote the note and meant it, but that during worship as we were praying for each other this lady prayed for me, and God already healed me. The whole congregation started praising God. The pastor just said that we would leave it like that for the moment. After preaching he asked me to come up anyway so he could anoint me, and I had no problem with that. Many people went forward, and many were falling under the Spirit.

On the way home I found out that my Aunt, who had taken me there, was mad at me and would not speak to me because during the time of prayer I didn't pray with her. She missed the entire miracle that the Lord had done because of her selfishness. I was so sad for her.

Immediately upon entering my Aunt's house all the pain came back again. I was so mad. I went straight to my bedroom, shut the door and started yelling at the devil. I said, *"Who do you think that you are trying to steal my healing? God has healed me and I am healed! Now get out in Jesus' name!"* Immediately all the pain left and never came back. Don't believe his lies!

That night UPS called me to come to work the next day, and I had to go to the store that night, which meant another eighteen hour shift. My Aunt just looked at me, because she knew how sick I was the day before. I just said to her, *"Hey, if I'm healed then I'm healed, and I can work again."* She just said, *"We'll see."* To their shock and amazement, I was totally fine after that. With those two jobs I earned just enough money to get me to England where Reinhard's brother and his wife were on vacation. I could ride back to Austria with them. It worked out perfectly.

The Married Me

Chapter 8 – The Adventure Begins
Minus How Much!?

I arrived in Austria four weeks prior to the wedding date so that all of our paperwork could be processed before the actual wedding. On the day of the wedding, as we arrived at the registrar's office, we were informed that the paperwork had not returned yet and therefore, we could not go through with the ceremony. We just decided to get the church ceremony from Reinhard's dad, who was a pastor, and after the honeymoon to get the official wedding done. But just about ten minutes before the wedding was supposed to have started, the paperwork came through. We therefore got married legally before we went away on our sixteen-day honeymoon.

Nobody from my family came to the wedding. In fact, there were only a handful of friends from England who came to be with us, plus all of Reinhard's dad's church members, of whom I knew no one. I didn't have anyone to walk me down the aisle so I asked my (at that time, future) father-in-law if he would, and he did. Then he went in front and married us. I didn't even understand the ceremony because it was all in German. At one point I whispered to Reinhard, *"What's going on?"* To which he replied, *"Take my hand, and when I squeeze it say, 'Ich Will'."* What? You don't understand that? Neither did I at the time. It means, *"I will."* That was strange to me because in the States we say, *"I do."*

Then we drove to England in two days and flew to Crete for sixteen days half-board at a four star hotel, which Reinhard received as a gift from a missionary who didn't even have the money himself to pay for it. The Lord told him to pay a good honeymoon for us. But *after* he paid for our honeymoon the Lord gave him all the money back.

We arrived back in Austria at the beginning of winter, which actually turned out to be one of the worst winters in Austria in the previous seventy years. We didn't get much snow that winter but the temperatures went down to -27 C! A girl growing up in California had never even realized such cold could even exist! There were many weeks when I didn't even leave the apartment except to go to the meetings and run home as quickly as I could. That happened many years when I was in Austria. I called it my *'winter hibernation'*.

After we returned home and were getting ready to go to bed the first night, suddenly Reinhard opened the window! I thought he was crazy! I asked him what he was doing and rushed to shut the window. He said he always slept with the heater off and the window open for fresh air. Fresh air at -27 C?! There was no way that was going to be possible. But he convinced me that it was healthier to sleep when the room temperature is cooler. I grew up in California with the heat on at night! But I agreed to try it his way.

The next morning I had a bad sore throat and could hardly talk. Then he agreed that we would do it my way the next night, which meant heat on and window closed. The next morning he woke up with a sore throat and could hardly talk. This was going to be some marriage! Finally we decided on a compromise: the window stayed open until 0 degrees Celsius but no heat; below 0 the window remained shut – but still no heat. It finally worked out.

After being married for a few months, Reinhard decided it was best for me to go to a university to learn German properly instead of having to struggle for so many years like many foreigners he had met. He sent me to Graz (a city an hour's drive away) to live with his parents for one semester.

I went to the university there to study 8am-5pm Monday through Friday and only went home on the weekends. When we signed up for the second semester, I was already pregnant with our first son (a miracle! – considering the distance). The second semester I rode daily with another couple who also lived in our area and were also from our Bible school. They had come to Austria to plant churches. NOW I wished I had listened to my Spanish teacher and had started taking German classes in high school! In the end it took me about four years to become fluent in German.

Many things happened in that first apartment to increase my faith. One day when my son was less than two years old, I stubbed my baby toe really hard against the corner of a wall. I went down in pain and tears came automatically, even though I wasn't crying. My son came over to me and laid his hands on me and said, *"Owie (that's baby talk for Ow - short for ouch - or pain) go, in Jesus name. Amen. All better Mommy, you can get up now."* I didn't want to discourage his faith, even though I still felt the pain. But I got up and took a step, and as soon as I did all the pain left me. It always helps to teach your children by example. He just did what I had always done when he got hurt.

Chapter 9 – Vicious Attacks
Daniel's Fevers

I noticed, a lot of times that the devil attacks the youngest or weakest ones in a family, if he can't seem to get to the stronger ones. In our family it was no different. The children and I were often under some kind of spiritual attack, usually physically.

One day when Daniel, our older son, was about eight months old he suddenly had a very high fever, which came upon him from one minute to the next. Thinking about it later, I remembered that it had also coincided with an immunization that he had for measles a few days prior to the sudden fever. He could also have been getting his first tooth at the time.

The fever came upon him so quickly that his temperature went up to 42 degrees Celsius (which is 107.6 Fahrenheit) in the space of just a few minutes. It went up so rapidly that his little body went into a seizure, and he stopped breathing for a minute or two. His lips turned blue, and his hands were clenched up tightly over his head. I had taken him into the bedroom to change his diaper just as it happened. We had two guests visiting us at the time from the USA. I yelled for Reinhard to come quickly, and he ran to see what was happening when he heard the tone of my voice. He then quickly ran to the bathroom and got me a cold towel to put on our son's head.

Then he called the ambulance and told them what was happening. He called his brother to come and get the guests. The ambulance building was right next door to our house, and his brother lived on the other side of the ambulance building, so everyone arrived at our apartment within minutes.

They put Daniel and me in the back of the ambulance and tried to get oxygen on him. Reinhard followed behind in our car. On the way to the hospital, they had to pull over because the technician in the back with me couldn't get the oxygen to work. The driver had stopped to come to the back to help. Reinhard started to panic a bit when he saw that they pulled over, and the driver went to the back to do something. But he motioned to Reinhard that it was nothing serious. They got the oxygen working, and we carried on to the hospital, which was about a fifteen minute drive.

Once at the hospital they wouldn't let me in the room with him. They said that since he was without oxygen for a minute or a little longer they would have to do a spinal tap on him to make sure that he didn't have meningitis.

A spinal tap is where the person has to be conscious, and they stick a long needle into the spinal cord to get out some of the fluid to test it. I have heard from someone (an adult) who has had to have them on occasion that they would not wish them on their worst enemy because they are so painful. Imagine the effect on an eight-month old baby!

Once I heard Daniel start screaming in agonizing pain, and there was not one thing I could do to help him, I started running as far away from the room as I could so I wouldn't hear him scream, crying as I ran. I had to get pretty far away from the room before I couldn't hear the sounds anymore. I found out later that Reinhard forced his way into the room to be with our son, which I had no idea I could have done, or of course I would have too. But I probably would have made them stop since they were hurting him so badly. That is probably why they did not allow mothers to go in there with their children.

Later they said they wanted to keep him in the hospital for a few days for observation. I also found out later (many years later), that they told Reinhard that because of lack of oxygen to the brain, he would probably have epilepsy or be mentally handicapped now for the rest of his life. Of course, Reinhard immediately took authority over the *"curse"* spoken over our son by the medical staff, and to this day he is extremely intelligent and has no medical condition what-so-ever. Thank you Jesus!

After they put him in a regular room, they told me I couldn't stay with him overnight because the special mother-child rooms they had were all being used. They had to put him in a room with other children, and I wouldn't be allowed to stay in that one. I had to leave that night and come back in the morning. Since he was a baby, they put him in a crib, but it had very high sides to it that reminded me of a cage. His fever was so high that he was shivering in just a diaper and he seemed cold, but they didn't give him anything to keep warm. They just left him there, crying. Again, my heart broke as I had to leave him there, with him not being able to understand what was happening and why mommy could not stay with him.

He only had to stay one or two nights, but when I did bring him home he was extremely fearful every time I had to put him down for bed at night. He would have something similar to panic attacks. I had just read previously in a magazine or book about babies, that something similar had happened to one family and the Lord had told them to ask the child for forgiveness for abandoning him. Even though the baby was not able to understand the words or what was being said, his spirit would understand and respond.

I asked Daniel to forgive me for leaving him when he needed me and for abandoning him to those *"mean"* people. Of course, he didn't answer me or understand anything I was saying, but his spirit did. And when I put him to bed that night, and every night after that again, he was peaceful again and had no more attacks or panic of any sort.

Another time Daniel had to be rushed to the hospital, also with a very high fever, and again the doctors said that he would probably have meningitis, but no more spinal taps. He had to stay in the hospital again, this time for longer, about four-six days, I can't remember exactly. Reinhard stayed with him in the hospital in one of those special rooms I had mentioned before. I couldn't be there with him that time because I had to take care of our second son at home. I did go and visit him a few times though, but little children and babies are not usually allowed to visit in the hospitals there so his brother couldn't see him.

One day a friend came over looking for Reinhard, and when I told him where he was and what was happening, he immediately went to the hospital and stayed with them that whole day, and they both prayed continually for Daniel. The doctors wanted to put an IV in Daniel as soon as he arrived to be able to put fluids in him, or some kind of medicine if the tests proved that he needed some.

But Reinhard wouldn't let them stick him with any needles, because he said that Daniel had suffered enough already. It was very difficult for them to get the needles in properly, and it took them many tries to succeed, in previous attempts, so that is why Reinhard refused to let them this time. The doctors informed him that by the afternoon they would be back, and that they were definitely going to put the IV in if Daniel's fever hadn't gone down by then.

Reinhard and our friend kept praying, and before the doctor returned the fever was gone. They released Daniel the next morning because they said that there was nothing else wrong with him. Naturally they said they had no explanation for what happened to him being able to heal so quickly. But everyone who knows Jesus knows exactly what happened.

Chapter 10 – Problems and Provision

Reinhard had some awful jobs while we lived in that first apartment. One time he was an aerial photo salesman. He was selling pictures of people's houses that were photographed from a plane or helicopter. They were very expensive, so he rarely sold any. As the money kept dwindling he also went out and sold newspapers during the night. Sometimes I went along in the car to keep him company. One time he hadn't sold anything for a long time and the money was gone. I used to budget very carefully and never spent even ten cents that we didn't need to spend. But when it was gone there was nothing left. I was five months pregnant at the time with our first son.

When Reinhard came home that night, I told him that we were out of money and out of food. Our cupboards were completely bare. I didn't mention that pregnant women were supposed to eat. I didn't want to put the extra pressure on him. Not only that, but a friend from England had called me earlier and asked if we were going to be home for the weekend because he wanted to come and visit. It was a 1,800 km (about 1,118 miles) drive for him. But he asked me not to tell Reinhard, because he wanted to surprise him. Now we were expecting guests, and I literally had nothing to set before them to eat.

From somewhere deep within, Reinhard said to me, *"Well, can't God open the storehouses of heaven and pour out a blessing on us?"* I agreed he could, so we went to bed, a little bit hungry. The next morning the doorbell rang and Reinhard was surprised. When he answered he was even more surprised to hear our English friend on the intercom (we lived on the fourth floor). The friend asked if he could come up and Reinhard let him in.

After talking for a few minutes, he asked Reinhard to come down to the car with him, well, come down with *them* actually because he had brought a friend. The car was filled in the trunk and the back seat with food. His youth group had been saving up stuff for us for months, and on that exact night he felt he should bring it to us. I called my sister-in-law to come and divide the food with me, and that afternoon our cupboards were sagging under the weight of the food. Later I even had some missionaries from New Zealand who came to visit, and I fed them with some of that food as well. The storehouses were truly opened.

The jobs still weren't working out so well, and we got a few months behind on our rent. Then the bank decided not to pay any more payments for us and blocked our account. It was at that time that the girl from the Air Force in England, who had asked me all those years ago if I wanted to go to church with her, decided to come visit us. She stayed for a week or two, but we never once mentioned our financial needs to her. In fact, we never mention our financial needs to anyone except God. That has been our rule since we first got married, and it has worked quite well. The night or so before she was to leave, she told us that she had sold a house in England and was praying about it, and God told her she should give 10% to us. She did, and it totally cleared our bank account and paid the outstanding rents! God always takes care of His children.

Our Own House with Its Own ~~Problems~~ Opportunities

Soon our second son was born, and our sixty-eight square meter (about 700 sq ft) apartment was too small for us. I kept asking Reinhard to move to a house. Finally he found one about thirteen km (eight miles) outside of the town we were in. It was in a small village of about three hundred people, who never accepted us because we were not born and raised in that very Catholic village.

One day, the wind blew some old plastic plant pots from our yard into the neighbor's yard behind us. She actually had a reputation for being a grumpy woman. When she caught me outside one day, she threw them angrily back over the fence and complained about us messing up her yard, or something like that. I made a rude comment back to her about her grumpiness being well established in the village or some similarly disrespectful comment. She was even angrier at me, and then this tension between us made me want to move out of the village.

Have you heard about the psychological

terms, *fight or flight*? It puts people in one of two categories: those who flee from unpleasant circumstances or even danger and those who stand up and fight in them. I was definitely a flight person. Every time something unpleasant was around, I wanted to run away. But in this case the Lord wanted me to learn to stand and fight – His way.

He told me to go and ask her to forgive me for what I said. Oh, I remember that lesson too well. The next time I saw the lady, I called her to the fence, and told her I was sorry for saying mean things to her and asked her to forgive me. She suddenly became so nice to me and was so until the day we moved away four years later. The tension was gone, and I no longer wanted to run away. We need to learn to fight - God's way.

As soon as we moved into that house and until our youngest son was two years old, Reinhard worked at a company that had him travel and visit stores in half of Austria every week. That meant that I was basically alone with the children, cut off from anyone for two whole years. He only came home on Friday nights, spent the evening with the family, and then on Saturdays he would go down into the basement and pray most of the day. Sundays he would be traveling for the different church plants that were going on. In Kindergarten one time the teacher asked Daniel what his father did for a job and he replied, *"He goes down to the basement to pray."*

One day, after two years of practically total isolation, I just could not take it anymore. In my desperation I fasted three days asking God to do something. Because of my loneliness I couldn't promise Him I wouldn't do something I would hate myself for afterwards.

About a week later Reinhard called me to tell me that his boss called him to come to the office. He was worried that he might get fired. I was trying to stay positive, so I mentioned something about him maybe getting a promotion. And indeed, the boss was so happy with his work that he wanted to fire the other man who was taking care of the other half of Austria and give Reinhard the whole country! That meant that we would literally never see him again. He turned the offer down, realizing that this meant that it was time for a change. The boss begged him not to quit, and then offered him an 8-5 job in the city an hour's drive from us (Graz, where I studied German) which meant he could be home every evening. He would have been the manager of a big department store with hundreds of employees under him. He started the three month training, but after one month he quit, realizing that wasn't what the Lord wanted him to be doing.

He asked me to pray about it and see what I felt the Lord was saying. As I prayed I got the verse from 1 Corinthians 15:58 (in the New International Version),

> *"Therefore, my dear brothers and sisters, stand firm. Let nothing move you. Always **give yourselves fully to the work of the Lord**, because you know that your labor in the Lord is not in vain"* (Emphasis mine).

I told him what I felt God had said: that it was time to go full-time into the ministry and forget about secular work. The problem with that was that none of the churches were big enough yet to support even one minister full time. He got a little angry with me because as the man, he felt the burden to provide for the family. He asked me if I was going to supply what we needed to live, and I told him no, but that the Lord would.

About a week after that, we had a friend from our Bible school who was from Wales (in Great Britain) come to visit us. He was going to preach on Sunday, and Reinhard would translate. The main verse that he used to preach from was 1 Corinthians 15:58 from the NIV.

Reinhard had to repeat that verse many times during the sermon, and as I was telling him with my eyes something like, *"See, God is really telling you that."* He kept answering with his eyes, *"I know, I know. OK!"* The next week he quit his job, and for the next two years we lived without an income and saw some wonderful miracles and provision from our incredible heavenly Father.

One day the heating oil ran out, which we used to heat the water and the air temperature in the house. The inside temperature went down to thirteen degrees C (fifty-five degrees F). We were wearing coats in the house, and heating water on an electric stove to bathe the children in the sink. They loved it. Reinhard was gone at that time, probably taking care of the other churches, but I just knew that the Lord would provide oil for us. The next day it snowed. This was in March so snow was not usual but happened occasionally.

I stood firm in my belief that my heavenly Father would take care of us. A few days later Reinhard checked one of our bank accounts and there was a mysterious deposit on there. Nobody really knew where it came from, but it was enough money to buy five hundred liters of oil.

The problem now was that our tanks were for one thousand liters (we had three tanks) and no company wanted to come out and only give us half a tank. Finally we found one that did, and it was warm again in the house. I think that night I took a hot bath.

Chapter 11 - The Good Old Days
Full House

We call the days when we lived in that village the *Good Old Days,* because they contain so many wonderful memories of so many lives that we have touched and lives that have touched ours. That was the time that the church did a lot of evangelizing in our town, and we ended up having a lot of people living or staying with us.

The first ones who got saved and delivered were two drug addicts. The man was on heroine for ten years, and God set him free overnight. He had tried ten times before through rehab clinics to get free, but always ended up going back to heroine. One morning when they woke up there was no food in the house (ex-drug addicts can eat a lot!) and they kind of complained that they were hungry and there was no food in the fridge. Reinhard gathered us all together, and we stood in a circle in our dining room and he prayed. He told God that we were hungry and thanked Him for His generous provision for us. As he was praying he heard a car door shut. He quickly said, *"Amen"* and ran down the stairs to see who was there. There was no car in sight, but instead a big box of groceries sat in front of our door.

Our ex-drug addict (new family member) knew of some brothers whose mother was crazy, and again was in a mental institution. She kept going in and out. The boys were about eighteen and twenty at the time. They were sitting at home hungry and alone. So we took them in too. When I asked the eighteen year old if he wanted a drink, he looked at his brother to see what he should answer. He was not capable of making a decision on his own. It seemed that the mother had nine children, some of whom had already killed themselves, as were these two brothers planning to do the day we rescued them.

Her husband beat her regularly, so one day she decided to put poison in his food to kill him, but he didn't come home for dinner that night. In her desperation she called on the power of satan to help her kill her husband. Satan came alright, but instead he took over her whole family. When we went to the boys' apartment, we discovered recordings of each of the boys talking on individual cassettes. Throughout the recording the voices changed, even though it was only them on each recording. They were totally demon possessed. That was the beginning of many demon exorcisms over the next year or so. The younger brother ended up living with us for the next five years. The older one wasn't really interested in Jesus, only what he could get from us. The day we were sending him home his remark was, *"There was enough good stuff in my old life as well."* Sadly, within a few years he died.

Demons, Demons Everywhere – Literally

Our new family members (the ex-drug addicts) asked me if they could go and visit her sister, so they went for the day. As soon as they got there they called me in panic. It seemed the sister was being choked to death by a demon. I had called Reinhard, who told me to call our new worship leader, a young man who had been saved less than a year, and tell him to gather a few of the young people, who also had just recently gotten saved, and go over there to help her. Reinhard was in the south of Austria, and I had two small children, so we couldn't go. Once they got there they commanded the demon to stop choking her, and it stopped.

I contacted Reinhard and he said that they should bring the girl to our house. So far, we had the two ex-drug addicts, the two ex-satanists and then the demonized girl arrived. Another thing that was happening at exactly the same time was that our lead pastor, who was in England with his family, got into a terrible car accident. His whole family was unconscious, and the children were bleeding badly. They were in the hospital for at least a week. During that exact time, another pastor's daughter from England had flown to Austria to visit them, but they weren't there (because they were in a hospital in England). She was also staying in our house for a week or so.

We had the ex-satanists in the basement, the ex-drug addicts had their own small room, the pastor's daughter was on the sofa bed in the living room, and there was no room for the demonized girl, so I put her on the sofa bed next to the pastor's daughter. Reinhard asked me to ask the young worship leader if he would stay at our house that night so I wouldn't be alone with all those people – not that I was afraid. He slept in our bed, I slept on a mattress at the foot of the couch, and everybody else had their assigned places already.

Apparently, the problems had all started when this demonized girl began messing around with satanic stuff when she was twelve years old. She went to a séance where the table was levitating, and I am pretty sure that later she even had or tried to have sex with an animal. One day a witch told her, *"On your sixteenth birthday you will die."* She was young then and quickly forgot what the witch had said. It happened that just a few days before her sixteenth birthday the witch (whom she hadn't heard from in years) called her and said that she just wanted to wish her a happy sixteenth birthday. Then the girl remembered what the witch had said to her earlier. On her birthday she and her boyfriend had taken some drugs and were watching a horror movie. That was when the choking started and her sister arrived.

Going back to our house that night… Around midnight the demonized girl gets up and comes to me and tells me that she is hearing a voice saying that if our worship leader will read something to her from the Bible she will get better. I told her to go back to bed, and he can read to her in the morning. She insisted so in the end I got up and called our leader who told me he would be right there.

We went into the kitchen, and he started to read, and then she started to manifest. Then we started to cast the demon out in German, but I said *"Let's do it in English"* (because his English was perfect) and because I didn't want the girl to understand too much of what was going on in order to protect her a bit. Then the girl began to speak to us in perfect English, even though she had never learned a word of it before. After about an hour he asked me to make some coffee, because it looked like it would be a long night.

She kept going in and out, English then German. When she spoke in German we knew it was she and not the demon. We spent hours, and then I had the thought that I should call Reinhard because he had just finished a three week fast. I asked the worship leader if he thought I should call Reinhard and the demon replied, *"No!"* so I said, *"Thank you."* And went and called the pastor's house, where I thought he was staying, at four o'clock in the morning.

Reinhard said to get some of the young people together and bring her down to him, about a three to four hour drive away. She was not a very good girl on the drive down, and the poor youth who had only been saved for a few months were a bit out of their depth. They finally arrived and Reinhard made her (the demon) sit through an entire church service, but she was not quiet the whole time. On the recording of the meeting you could sometimes hear animal sounds coming from her or her screaming to Reinhard, *"I hate you!!"* in a deep guttural voice. Reinhard just said, *"I hate you too,"* and kept on preaching.

When I heard the recording later, at that part where she was saying how she hated him the hair on my arms stood up automatically. I had never experienced anything like that before or since. In the end he asked the worship leader to come and play something about the blood of Jesus. Then Reinhard walked up to the girl, pointed his finger at her and said, *"Out!"* She screamed loudly and was immediately totally free and couldn't speak another word of English. Later Reinhard asked her what she experienced when he said, *"Out"* and she said it was like light beams came out of his mouth and hit her and the demons left.

After that people kept calling us about demonized people who needed deliverance and asked if we could help. One time a group of us went to this one poor girl who had five to ten demons inside her. Throughout the conversation different ones would identify themselves, in different voices. At one point Reinhard stretched out his finger and started to command the demons to leave, and the girl bit his finger! He got it back, and in the end she did not want to be delivered, and we had to leave her there. It was very sad.

Youth Group

Now to return to our pastor and his family in England... Some of the youth who had just recently gotten saved decided that they wanted to come to our house every day and pray for the pastor and his family until they were completely well. We had regular prayer meetings daily for about a week or two. Afterwards the youth were all so used to hanging out at our house and that was how the youth group was formed. We became the unofficial, at first, youth leaders. They were there basically every day for about a year or two. More and more kept coming. Today those youth are now leaders in various churches.

During one of those youth meetings, in the course of the prayer time, Reinhard suddenly stopped praying and started prophesying over our four year old son, Daniel. He said, *"When he is sixteen years old he will move to the United States."* I almost started crying thinking about my baby leaving me. Later when it did come time for us to move to the States, one of the youth from that time called us. We hadn't heard anything from her in years. She asked us if it was true that we were moving to the States, and we confirmed that it was. Then she asked us how old Daniel was, and we told her he was sixteen, and why did she want to know? She then reminded us of the prophecy spoken over him when he was four that he would move to the States when he was sixteen. We had forgotten all about it. He *was* moving, but we were going with him!

But long before we moved to the States we moved two other times within Austria. One time we lived in the town where the lead pastor lived, about fifteen minutes' drive from us. It just made it easier to all be in the same town and the schools were better for the boys there. It was while we were living in that town that we got a dog, a big, white Golden Retriever. He was beautiful. We had taken him to obedience school too, so he was very well behaved. Some good and bad things happened there.

Chapter 12 – Attacks Continue
Christopher's Lungs

One night when our son Christopher was only about eight months old, Reinhard and I left both boys with our sister-in-law while we went to start a cell group (small group, life group, whatever you call it) in a town with no Christian witness. Both boys were in perfect health when we left. After the meeting we came home separately because Reinhard drove someone else home before coming home himself.

When I arrived at our house I asked my sister-in-law if everything was ok, expecting to her to say that it was. Instead, she said that it was, except for Christopher's cough. I was surprised because he had no cough when we left him.

I did not really think too much about it until shortly after she left when I heard a strange sound coming from our boys' bedroom. As I got closer to hear what the sound was, I discovered that it was Christopher gasping and trying to breath. I quickly grabbed him up out of his crib and went to the kitchen with him so he would not wake up Daniel, his older brother, who was only about two years old at the time.

Once in the kitchen I tried to call the house where Reinhard was (remember, that was a long time before cell phones even existed), but he had already left. All of a sudden, Christopher started gasping for breath again, and I didn't know what to do. He seemed like he would choke to death any second, right there in my arms. In a moment of panic I just said very forcefully, *"In the name of Jesus, breath!"* Instantly he drew in a deep breath. Then I thought to myself, *"Oh, ok, now I know what is happening here."*

I realized he was under a spiritual attack, which was probably directly connected to our starting that home group in the town we were just in. There is a lot of demonic activity in Austria. That was the beginning of a seven year spiritual battle for his total deliverance and healing.

Reinhard was gone many days and nights during those times leaving me alone to face the situation. Sometimes he left with a heavy heart not wanting to leave me alone with the boys. But we both knew that if he was taking care of the Lord's work, the Lord would take care of us, so he left. Sometimes I even had to force him to go. We both knew he had to leave. I never wanted to be the cause of him not doing the Lord's will, so I always encouraged him to go. It was totally different than when he was doing it just for money. I also said that people in the military leave their families for many months at a time and they only do it for their country; how much more should we be doing it for the Lord?

After that initial night in the kitchen, I spent many nights next to Christopher's bed (yes, it usually always only occurred at night), praying and trying to calm him so he wouldn't choke to death. When Reinhard was home Christopher would usually go to daddy to help him. (When he was old enough to walk he would come to our bedroom to get help).

He even had to go to the hospital on a number of occasions and had inhalers he was supposed to use whenever an *attack* came on. Any time there was a change in weather we could be almost certain Christopher was going to have some kind of choking reaction to it, and he usually did.

At first, the doctors said he would outgrow it by the time he was seven, but then they changed their minds and said there was no cure for him, and that he would have to live with inhalers for the rest of his life. His lungs were underdeveloped and his *larynx* (the organ of voice production, containing the vocal cords) was too narrow.

It is so heartbreaking to watch your children suffer, especially when you feel so helpless, and they keep looking to you to help them somehow. Everything in us parents wants to help them any way we can, even to the point of wishing we could take their ailments upon ourselves to relieve them of the pain and suffering. We would if there was any way such a thing could be possible. But we can thank our Jesus because that is exactly what He has done for every one of us!

After many years of watching my son suffer, it started to wear me down, and I couldn't watch it any longer. One night when he was having another attack I felt like giving up. I didn't think I could face another day of his suffering. I remember praying that night, *"Lord, You love him much more than I do, and I know you don't want him to suffer like this. I can't do this anymore, especially on my own."* I said, *"I am going to sleep and going to trust you to take care of him, because you can do it better than I, and you love him more than I do anyway."* Our bedrooms were right next to each other so I could hear every gasp of breath he took. But I went into my bedroom and put my pillow over my head. And even to my own surprise, I went to sleep.

When I woke up in the morning I was very scared to open his bedroom door for fear that he might be dead. I put my hand on the doorknob and hesitated, thinking about all the things that could possibly happen to me if he would be dead: they would prosecute me for negligence against my child; I would have guilt for the rest of my life for letting my son die; I was trying to bat away thoughts about what the people in church, my husband, doctors, or anybody else would say when they found out.

Of course, all this happened within a

split second of thought, and then I entered the room. It was quiet. I went over to his bed and put my hand near his nose and mouth to see if I could feel his breath, all the time holding mine. He was alive. I left the room quickly and thanked the Lord for taking care of him. Suddenly, just as I shut the door to their room, I heard the voice of the Lord so loudly in my spirit, *"Even if he would have died in the night, my love for you would not have changed."* I started crying and confessing, *"Lord, I don't understand your love."*

One night many years later, when Christopher again came and stood next to daddy to help him because he couldn't breathe, Reinhard woke up and told him to go back to bed. He would get his medicine and bring it to him. That night a deep compassion gripped Reinhard like never before. He went down on his knees on our kitchen floor and interceded for our son, like he had never done before, (not that we had never interceded for our son before, we had, many times). That night God answered Reinhard's prayer and healed Christopher. When Reinhard went to his bed with the medicine he was already sleeping peacefully.

The next day he was fine.

The next time Reinhard was the one who took him to the doctor, and the doctor kept hitting his machine and saying that something was wrong with it because it was impossible for there to be such an increase in Christopher's lung pressure. Reinhard and Christopher just smiled and looked at each other. Once outside Christopher looked up at his daddy and said, *"We know what happened, don't we daddy? Jesus healed me."* Reinhard just replied, *"Yes son, He did."* And he was healed from that day on. Never give up on expecting your miracle from God. We don't know why it takes longer sometimes for the answer to come, but we do know, the answer comes, if you don't give up your faith.

Chapter 13 – The Front Lines Are Moving
Time to Move to the Capital of Vienna

When the whole leadership team decided it was time to move to Vienna, the capital of Austria, I was reluctant. I had grown up in a big city, and they were full of dangers that small towns didn't have. I was trying so hard to protect my sons from any unnecessary dangers.

At one point my brother-in-law, who was one part of the leadership team, said to me that I didn't need to hear God say anything to me, I just needed to follow my husband wherever he went. I told him that God had spoken to me my whole Christian life, and I didn't believe He would stop now just because I was married. (You know the *'My sheep hear my voice'* verse? [John 10:27]) I fully believed that God would speak to me about us having to move, or preferably not, as I was hoping to hear.

Very shortly afterwards the Lord said so clearly to me, *"The front lines are moving to Vienna. Are you going?"* Since I had prayed that prayer so many years ago in England that I wanted to be on the front lines of the battle for the Lord, I didn't see any other possibility but to move. In truth, even though I said I trusted the Lord for my boys, I was still scared about them being in a big city.

We lived in two different places in Vienna. In the first apartment a young girl we were friends with, and who also lived in Vienna, came to help me clean out some of the cupboards so we could move our stuff in. While we were cleaning I heard the voice of the Lord so clearly say, *This is the daughter I am giving you for the one you lost all those years ago.* When I started to think about it, I thought that the child that I had aborted would have been the exact same age as she was at that moment. But until the Lord said that, I had no idea it had been a girl. I started to cry. Then I told her what the Lord said, and we both cried together. To this day she is truly my daughter in the Lord. We are still very close.

Throughout the years our leadership team of six used to have many character and relational problems with each other. It seemed most of their problems somehow involved me. Out of the six of us, I was the only one who did not grow up in a Christian home. They found me very difficult to deal with. It was no surprise that the very first prophecy I ever received started with the words, *"You have always been the odd one out…"*, meaning that no matter what other people were like or doing, I was basically *totally* opposite or different from them. Let me give you one example: In my teenage years all my friends were listening to the Beatles, Lead Zeppelin, Rolling Stones, etc. I was listening to Oldies music from the 1950's-60's.

After about eleven years of leadership problems, something came up causing problems again. This time it was like something happened inside of me. I was tired of forgiving them and especially always having to ask them to forgive me. I knew the verses about having to forgive those who do things against us (forgiving 70 X 7 for example) and the one in Matthew 18:33-34,

> *"Shouldn't you have had mercy on your fellow servant just as I had on you? In anger his master **handed him over to the jailers to be tortured**, until he should pay back all he owed. **That is how my heavenly Father will treat each of you***

unless you forgive your brother or sister from your heart" (Emphasis mine).

But at that time I was willing to take the risk with the torturers (or tormentors, as it said in the version I was reading at the time – NIV).

That night I had a dream. It was of a long train that was like a moving village. People lived permanently on this train. The last car of the train was like a store where the people who lived on the train could buy the things they needed. The store was run by a family: husband, wife and two older sons. They were like hillbillies. The sons were very rude to the customers.

One day someone on the train had enough of their rudeness and went back to the store and locked the door. They took the two sons and tied them up and hung them upside down from the ceiling of the train. Then this person took a knife and cut their throats and watched them bleed to death, choking on their own blood. Afterwards they went out the door and locked it and went back to their own train car. When the train pulled into the next station there was blood flowing out from the last wagon or car. Then I heard a child's voice on the platform (who I recognized to be the voice of my son Christopher when he was little), who said, *"Mommy did it!"* At that moment I jerked awake. Immediately a scripture verse went through my mind, *"Anyone who hates his brother is a murderer."* I then thought, *"That is quoted wrong."* I got my Bible and looked it up and found it in 1 John 3:15. It was quoted correctly. It says,

> *"Anyone who hates a brother or sister is a murderer, and you know that no murderer has eternal life residing in him."*

I immediately realized that no matter what other people have done to me, if I hate them, in God's eyes it is the same as the most heinous murder. You see, my lack of forgiveness turned very quickly to bitterness and then just as rapidly turned into hatred. I had to once again ask them to forgive me, this time for my hatred of them.

We moved one more time in Vienna. It was right next door to the school the boys would be attending. That was great for me because then

I could keep an eye on them. I would see them during the breaks, and if they were sitting on the bench alone and no one was talking to them or playing with them, I would start to cry and intercede for them to have good friends to play with. One day I came home from somewhere, and they were both standing outside, and Christopher was crying. I asked him what had happened, and he told me he had just gotten beaten up.

I went inside with them, and later I was angry at God. I told Him that He had promised to take care of my boys and now this happened. When I asked Him why He didn't protect them, I heard Him say very clearly, *"I couldn't, because you were in the way."* In my desperation to protect my children I was blocking the protection of the Lord over their lives. We need to care and protect our children, but if we think that their protection is in our hands, then we are blocking God from doing His part to protect them. We need to let go a little and trust more.

One funny thing happened in our new apartment. I had been talking to Reinhard about being open to dreams from the Lord. He was reluctant, but he did pray about it. One night Reinhard had a dream that our dog (who always slept with our son Christopher) had diarrhea and was trying to get out of the room to go to the front door. Reinhard said he could see the color of the poop and everything. Then he woke up and thought, *"What a stupid dream."* Then he went back to sleep.

In the morning when he got up, he told me about the dream, and I told him he needed to go and check the room. He went to check on the dog and the boys. When he entered Christopher's room there was everything (up to the exact color of poop he had seen) exactly as it was in the dream. He came and told me that I needed to go and clean it up, which I normally always did if the dog had an accident. But in this case I said to him, *"You had the dream and ignored God. You need to go and clean it up."* He couldn't really argue with that. I think God was just trying to teach him to hear His voice in dreams. He learned very quickly after that to pay attention to his dreams.

Chapter 14 - Dying to see the U.S.

Defying the Devil

A very dear friend of ours had just paid for us to fly to the US to stay with her for a while. Just before we were ready to leave, I got very sick, and Reinhard had to take me to the hospital. It was in front of a nurse that he told me we needed to cancel our trip to the States. The nurse told him that wasn't necessary. They would just give me some antibiotics through an IV (into the veins), and then send me on after them. The nurse and I convinced him to take the boys and go on ahead.

But instead of getting better I was getting worse. One day I looked out the window of the hospital and saw a plane flying by and thought, *"Here I am dying and my family is far away in the States."* Then after about a week I decided that enough was enough. I gathered together all my energy, got my Bible and went out of the room to find a quiet place to ask God what was going on. I remember so clearly that I started reading somewhere in Isaiah, I think, God was saying something like how terrible you are, your sins are horrific, you deserve to die, etc., and I remember thinking, *"But God, what did I do?"* I was sitting there all confused, wondering what horrible thing I had done when I had this feeling of a big face next to me smiling and it said, *"Keep reading."*

So I read into the next chapter something about sharing something with my people's children, or something like that. Then I said to God, *"But my people's children are the Americans,"* and God said to me, *"Exactly."* Then I said, *"Oh, so I am going to America?"* And He confirmed that I was. That day the doctor came in to check on me and decided that maybe I was still sick because of the medicine they were giving me and crossed it all off my chart. That night I awoke and heard God say, *"I healed you a long time ago. They have been keeping you sick with their medication."* Then I replied, *"Oh is that why you had the doctor cross it all off my chart?"* Then I went back to sleep and started to get better the next day.

Soon they released me, and I flew to the States. But on the way, in my weakened state, I started getting worse again. I told my friend to have a wheelchair ready for me when I got there and didn't think I would make it, to be honest.

Once I arrived at her house I went straight to bed and stayed there for about a week, not eating and barely drinking anything and getting weaker by the day. My friend and Reinhard were seriously worried that I was going to die, so independently of each other and without talking about it, they both started fasting for me.

After about three days her pastor came and asked if he could pray for me. I let him. The next day I started to think to myself, *"What would I be doing right now if I wasn't sick?"* I thought, *"I would be eating Cheetos."* (Don't judge me.) I got up and took out a Cheeto from the bag and said, *"Devil, I eat this in defiance of you!"*, and from that time on I started to get better.

I remember Reinhard's face that morning when he came into the room and saw me eating Cheetos and exclaimed, *"What are you doing?!"* I told him I was eating those in defiance of the devil. The next day we went hiking up a small mountain, and I had a steak dinner in the evening and everything was fine. It was after that visit to my friend's that we flew to Los Angeles, on the way home to Austria, so my family could see where I grew up. And it was then that I finally got to see where my dad was buried.

Chapter 15 – Parting Ways
Leadership Problems – Again

The problems in the leadership intensified to such a point that it was decided we could not work together anymore, and that it would be better if we all separated. But since we were so heavily involved only in the church work, we basically knew no non-Christians. And so overnight we had essentially just lost all of our friends. And strangely enough, in the middle of all the turmoil, both Reinhard and I had total peace. We didn't understand what was happening, but we knew that somehow God was in the middle of it all. Daniel was fourteen when that happened, and of course it hit him very hard. Christopher, who was twelve, just rolled with it, not letting it bother him too much (at least outwardly).

Reinhard didn't want to be without a church, so we started attending another one in the city. It was a big international church with meetings Fridays to Sundays for five different groups: Philippinos, English speaking Africans, French speaking Africans, German speaking, and English speaking. We decided to go to the

German speaking meetings. Reinhard knew the pastor of that congregation since the pastor and his wife had gotten saved, many years previously.

Everybody in the country who was a Christian knew Reinhard. Not too long after being there, they asked us to be leaders with them. Reinhard felt it wasn't right yet, but we did end up being home group leaders. Our home group meetings saw so many miracles and answers to prayers that people from other groups wanted to start coming to our meetings too.

Then one day God started speaking to us and releasing us to move on, again. The pastor did not want us to leave, but after we had shared with him how the Lord was leading us, he had to admit that it was God. Then he gave us his blessing to move on.

Chapter 16 – Totally Unexpected
A New Year

Suddenly it was New Year's Eve of 2003, and we asked a few close friends to come and pray with us into the New Year. As we were praying the Lord spoke to Reinhard, *"This will be a year of great change for you."* He told me what the Lord had said, and I was very happy because I was really ready for a radical change. Then the Lord said, *"This year you will move far away."* Reinhard told me what the Lord said further. I was thinking maybe we would move to Germany or even Brazil. Why Brazil?

How Brazil Started

Reinhard had been going to Brazil for some years already. It started when the father of the main pastor of our previous church (who lived in Italy) called his son in Austria and told him that they had this Brazilian pastor speaking there. He asked if we wanted to have him at our church. He came up, and Reinhard translated for him from English into German. His English was very bad but through some miracle (anointing?) Reinhard understood everything.

There was this heart connection between the pastor from Brazil and Reinhard. The pastor's name was Robson. He then asked Reinhard to come over to Brazil and minister in some of his *Sera Nossa Terra* churches in different cities. Reinhard started going over to Brazil in January 1996.

Around that time pastor Marcelo, who worked closely with Robson, moved to Portugal to start a work there. When he started to struggle in Portugal, because Europe is completely different from Brazil, Robson called Reinhard and asked him if he could go over to help him out. We went, and while we were there, Reinhard had a word for Pastor Marcelo about leaving the person he currently walked with and joining himself to another man. Pastor Marcelo had already been told by the Lord that he needed to leave Robson and join together with Pastor Aluízio who was starting Videira (or the Vine), but he didn't want to tell Robson that.

In the end Pastor Marcelo left *Sera Nossa Terra* and joined Videira (the Vine). A year or so later they invited Reinhard over to do the first conference for about six hundred people. It was in that meeting that Reinhard had such a strong prophetic word for Videira/Vine, the founding pastor Aluízio and his wife Márcia. It was also just before that same meeting where Reinhard thought it would be fine to drink the water from the faucets, and then he got diarrhea. After the meeting, he started to pray for the people, and we ended up praying for about three hundred people, until after one o'clock in the morning.

At one point during the prayers he accidentally pooped himself. He told me about it, and I said, *"So what are you going to do? All these people have been waiting for hours for you to pray for them; you can't stop now."* He replied, *"You don't understand, it is running down my leg."* But somehow I convinced him to keep going, and it was soon forgotten. A little while later, as he was prophesying, he started to fall asleep. I stomped on his foot, and he quickly woke up again and continued. His interpreter's eyes were rolling in the back of his head at times because he could hardly stay awake. That was our beginning experience with Videira/Vine.

A New Door

Anyway, returning to New Year's Eve, 2003. After the Lord had said that we would move far away, He then told Reinhard that we would move to the US. Then Reinhard told the Lord that He would need to tell me that. Reinhard told the Lord that I was Reinhard's wife but the Lord's daughter, and it was His job to speak to His daughter. Besides, he didn't want to tell me because he said that I always told him that I didn't want to live in the States again.

Four months later, in April, I was reading a book by Rick Joyner, who is a known prophet in the States, and who started MorningStar Ministries. The book was burning in my heart (but I didn't realize until later that it was the Holy Spirit burning in there), and I told Reinhard, *"I want to be a part of MorningStar."* As soon as I said that, the Lord said to Reinhard, *"That is where you are going."* He said to me, *"Ok, we are moving to the States."* I said, *"Don't mock me, I am serious."* He said, *"So am I. the Lord told me on New Year's Eve that we are moving to the States. Now he just told me where to go."* I said, *"Seriously?"*

But we didn't even know where MorningStar was located. I turned the book over that I was reading, and it said Moravian Falls, North Carolina. I tried looking it up on a map, but I couldn't find it. I said, *"Boy, this place is really small. It's not even on a map."* Little did I know at the time just how small it really was.

Only With a Green Card

Reinhard was determined to only go with a green card, the immigration status of a person authorized to live and work in the United States, and those were hard to come by after 9/11 and the twin tower attacks. We went to the American Consulate in Vienna to start the proceedings. They asked me how much money or assets I had, which according to them had to be at least $100,000. That was just in case if my husband got there and decided to apply for government assistance, I could pay the government back. We walked out of the Consulate, and I remember saying to Reinhard, *"Well, **that** door is closed."*

Then we read somewhere that we could get a sponsor who was someone in the States who had the money and would be willing to vouch for us and to pay the money back should we ever go on welfare. I thought of my friend who had paid for us to go over to the States a few years earlier and sent her a message and asked her. She said, *"Of course I will do it. I will do anything to get you guys closer."* Then I said to Reinhard, *"The door is open again."*

Then the Consulate started processing the paperwork and told us that we could not enter the US while they were in the process of doing the paperwork, which would take some months. We told them that we already had a trip booked in a few months' time, and they told us to cancel either the trip or the paperwork. But we didn't cancel the paperwork, and we still went to the States.

When we came back Reinhard had an interview with the Consulate director, and I asked him, *"What are you going to say when they ask you why you want to go?"* He answered, *"The Holy Spirit will tell me what to say when the time comes."* The day arrived for his interview, and he went in to talk to the lady. She began by asking him how long we had known each other and he said, *"Twenty years, married eighteen years"*.

Then she asked, *"And why do you want to go to the United States?"* He started to stammer and mumble and then finally said, *"Uh, I wanna go, my boys wanna go and my wife wants to go."* I call that his Holy Spirit-inspired answer. Then the lady smiled and said, *"Oh, I see, you just want a change, huh?"* Reinhard nodded in agreement not knowing what else to say. Afterwards she said, *"I see that you just had a birthday yesterday. Would you like the green card as a birthday present?"* Reinhard said, *"Pardon me?"* She replied, *"You heard me. Welcome to the United States of America. Sit down and wait and I will be right back with your paperwork."* When he left the building he called me and told me that he had all the paperwork for the green card. The card itself would be sent to an address in the US, and we had to pick it up there.

Chapter 17 - Sowing and Reaping
The Start of a Fantastic Discovery

I forgot to mention that while we were living in Vienna, we decided to start sowing our money. We gave tithes and offerings and gave to the poor, but we read about sowing and reaping (2 Cor 9:10)

> *"Now may He who supplies seed to the sower, and bread for food supply and multiply the seed you have sown and increase the fruits of your righteousness, "*

and wanted to start doing that too. When we started, we decided to sow one month's income into ministries or missionaries that the Lord would show us, but only in good soil, people who were already producing good things for the Lord or we could see were about to. We were just getting by month to month on the income that we had at the time, so it was a big step of faith for us to pledge one whole month's income over the course of a year.

We kept exact records of how much we gave and to whom and when (sowed) and how much we received (reaped) in a little book. We also agreed about everything beforehand and only gave if we both agreed. Some strange things happened as far as money coming in for us (reaping) was concerned.

One time we received some money from the heating company as a refund for heating costs for the apartment for the previous year. The only thing was, we hadn't lived in that apartment the year before, in fact, nobody did. It was empty for one whole year before we moved in, and it was new, so we were the first people to actually ever live in it. Reinhard called the company and tried to explain the situation to give them their money back. After about half an hour the girl on the other end of the phone said kind of grumpily, *"The computer says it is yours so it is yours!"*, and hung up the phone. We kept the money, thanked the Lord and marked it under reaping.

At one point towards the end of the year it looked like we were not going to be able to make our promise and give the whole month's salary. We informed the boys (who were around ten and twelve years old at the time) that there would be no Christmas presents that year (at that time we still celebrated Christmas), and they were ok about it. Giving to the Lord was more important than anything else. Then something happened, and we were able to pay the Lord what we promised and buy presents for the boys. God is so faithful. He even helps us give to Him when we are serious about it.

Sowing and reaping are still one of our favorite things to do, and you reap much more than investments and bank interest. Every year we always reaped much more than we sowed. The next year Reinhard said, *"How much should we sow this year?"* and I excitedly replied, *"Two month's salary?"* He immediately said, *"Are you crazy?"* I can't remember what we promised that year, but whatever it was I can assure you, we made our goal. And it keeps going up and up. In actual fact, our goal is now to give away 99% of our income and live on the 1%. We're getting closer.

Chapter 18 - In the United States
MorningStar Ministries

Once we moved to the States I ended up getting a job in the MorningStar warehouse, which is where the books, CD's, DVD's etc., are all stored to be shipped out when people write in for orders. It was fun and I really enjoyed it. And I got a lot of free books while I was there. In the end I must have had over three thousand books spread out throughout the house, as well as many I gave away to pastor friends and so on.

Then the warehouse moved from North Carolina to South Carolina, because they bought the old property from Jim Baker who had started some Christian theme park (PTL). The property had closed down years previously, and it was in great disrepair, so MorningStar got it very cheap. Then they decided to move the MorningStar headquarters from Moravian Falls, North Carolina down there to the new property in Ft. Mills, South Carolina. Today it is a beautiful place, with a hotel and conference center and a beautiful main street, etc.

But before they moved, I was doing some

cleaning jobs, and one of the jobs I had was for Rick Joyner's wife Julie, to clean their house. It was an amazing house, I can tell you. I think it had ten bedrooms and ten bathrooms plus all kinds of other rooms, even a prophetic room at the top where I guess Rick used to meditate and pray. It was very peaceful there.

After the move I became the buyer for all the products that the warehouse needed, a special job they created just for me. I used to call all the famous publishing houses and had to deal with them about orders for books, but the CD's I usually ordered directly from the artists themselves. It was a fantastic job. Reinhard remarked once that I had the best job in the world: I could talk on the phone all day and spend someone else's money. Who can argue with that? After that I became the church secretary for MorningStar, the Moravian Falls church. At that time there were four or five MorningStar churches spread throughout the State. I was the secretary for about nine months before I felt it was time to leave that job.

The funny thing was that the day after I quit, Reinhard lost his job and our son lost his job too. So 75% of our family income was lost overnight. But the Lord sustained us until we got other jobs and we lacked nothing during that time.

Chapter 19 - More Kids
Fostering

We felt led to move into a particular house, which was owned by a couple who attended MorningStar, and who were moving to Oregon, thousands of miles away. We rented it for a year, and then we had to decide if we wanted to buy it or move out so they could sell it. We both fasted and prayed about it. The Lord clearly told us to buy the house but not to pay more than a certain amount for it and a certain amount in monthly mortgage payments. The price the Lord told us was $10,000 less than what they were asking for the house.

We told them that we would have to move out because the house was worth what they wanted but that we could not afford that much. Then a few weeks later they contacted us and said that the Lord had spoken to them and said, *"Do you want the money or do you want a blessing?"* They decided they wanted the blessing and let us have the house for the amount we could afford. We also got a special deal with the bank and everybody (even the bank people) said they never heard of a deal like we got.

But while we were fasting about the house situation, the Lord also very clearly said to both of us independently, that we needed to start fostering children. I was ready to finally be done with taking care of children. Mine were now grown up, and I was eager to start traveling with Reinhard where he ministered.

In obedience to the Lord though, we started the process to become foster parents. The area we lived in had a high percentage of drug abuse, and the children were suffering greatly because of the habits of their parents. We ended up fostering seven troubled teenage boys over the course of the next five years. Many times they tried to get us to take girls too, but we refused because a troubled teenage girl would only have had to say that one of our sons touched her wrong or something like that and they, and maybe us too, would end up in jail. No thanks.

We lived in in a part of the country where the education level of most of the population was not very high. The whole time I had lived in the States growing up, I had never been to that part of the country before. Even the dialect took a while before I could understand some of them.

And the boys that we did take in had stories that would make you cry. But some of them accepted Jesus, and one even got baptized. I know we did a lot of good and could show them some of the Lord's love through our lives.

Chapter 20 - The Big 5–0!
Fifty Years and Still Going Strong

It was getting close to the time of Reinhard's fiftieth birthday. I told him he should do something special for his fiftieth, because he never really did anything that he wanted to do. For vacations and anniversaries he always did what I wanted to do, even though I kept trying to persuade him otherwise. He is selfless like that. He thought and thought for a long time, and then decided that he would invite his best friend and his family to come over from Austria and spend a month with us. The wife and kids would stay with me, and he and his friend would ride motorcycles for two weeks throughout the eastern part of the States. He told his friend, who also loved the idea, and they both started saving five years in advance.

The year finally came, and a few months beforehand a friend of ours from our church, who happened to be Brazilian, came to our home one evening. She told us that she would be moving to Florida, and when she said where she was moving, it was to the exact same city where

Pastor Marcelo now had a church. Reinhard said, *"I need to connect you with him. Let me call him."* So he called Marcelo, who answered the phone all groggily. When Reinhard asked him if he woke him up, because it was only eight o'clock in the evening, Marcelo answered, *"No, it is three in the morning. I am in Africa."*

Reinhard apologized and wanted to quickly hang up so he could go back to sleep, but Marcelo wouldn't let him. He told him that they were planning a conference in Florida, and all the leadership agreed that Reinhard should be the guest speaker. But they would not call him; they would wait for Reinhard to call them. And now he was. Reinhard said, *"Great. When is the conference?"* When Marcelo told him, it was exactly during part of the trip that had been planned for the last five years. Reinhard finally said, *"I'm sorry. I can't do it at that time."*

They talked a few more minutes, and then he hung up. When he explained everything to us, I said to him, *"Can't you see this is obviously God? You can't just say no like that."* He explained that he couldn't leave his friend hanging after he had been saving for five years. Then I said, *"Call him and see what he says."*

When Reinhard called him, his friend said, *"Who am I to stand in the way and the will of God?"* In the end they cut their ride short by five days or so, and both of them went to the conference. While they were in the first meeting the presence of the Lord was so strong that Reinhard was on the floor weeping before the Lord.

Then the Lord spoke clearly to him and said, *"Remember the time when you were a little boy and you said to me, 'Lord I will do anything you ask me to'? Does that still count?"* And Reinhard replied, *"Yes, Lord."* Then the Lord said to him, *"Then move to Brazil and help Videira fulfill their vision."* Then Reinhard added, *"You know that I will always obey You and do what You ask. But Lord, if this is really You, then I want You to open doors in Videira for me. I will not talk to any man or ask any person for an invitation".*

Beginning that very next month, and every month afterwards, at least one Videira/Vine church, somewhere in the world, contacted Reinhard and asked if he could preach at their church. This went on for quite a long time. When he came home from that conference in Florida he informed me that we were moving to Brazil. It was actually something I felt for a long time that we would do one day, so I wasn't surprised. Now we were just waiting on the timing of God again, as to when.

Chapter 21 - Boys!!
More Angels Appear

Having a house full of boys (men) can have its downside as well. For example, boys like to wrestle, a lot, all the time, even with their mother! In our house we went through *four* couches because of my boys, the foster kids and my husband wrestling in the living room. So two of the rules that were made were: 1) Take the wrestling outside on the grass where it is first of all softer and secondly, nothing can get broken, like furniture, etc. 2) If you break some body part on another person, and they have to go to the hospital to have it taken care of, the person responsible for sending the other person to the hospital had to pay for the hospital bills.

The reason for this one was simple. Most people then did not have health insurance, and just to walk into an emergency room at that time cost $700, before the doctor even looked at you! So everyone made sure to stop their wrestling or hurting the other before they were seriously injured.

One day I was in the kitchen and

Reinhard and Daniel, and I think one of our foster sons, were in there at the same time (our kitchen was a pretty decent size in that house). Suddenly, Reinhard jumped up on Daniel from the front and put his legs around Daniel's waist and was holding onto his neck. Daniel was holding onto Reinhard's back, and as they were messing around like that for a while, I asked them to please go outside before they knock off the kitchen machine or the microwave or break something else. Reinhard then let go of Daniel thinking Daniel was still going to be holding him. But at the same time Daniel let go of Reinhard thinking Reinhard was still going to be holding onto him. They both let go at the same time. At that time Daniel was full grown, meaning he was 6'1" (1m 86cm).

When they both suddenly let go of each other, Reinhard fell from a height of about three feet (one meter) straight onto a tiled floor flat on his back. In those days he was suffering from three herniated discs in his back (from which he has since been healed) and as he hit the floor, he just laid there and didn't move. I immediately thought of the herniated discs, and that he possibly broke his back. It looked like he was in a lot of pain, so I immediately bent over him and laid my hands on him and wanted to say, *"Jesus, help him"*, but the only thing that came out of my mouth was, *"Jesus, Jesus, Jesus, Jesus"* repeatedly. I tried to say something else but nothing else would come out.

Reinhard said that he wanted to get up and said to himself, *"Ok, get up now"*, but his body would not respond to the commands of his brain. He said he could not feel any part of his body, not even my hands on his stomach. He told me later that as I was just saying, *"Jesus"* suddenly he saw four angels that came down in a V-formation, two on each side of him. They put their wings under his back, and after a few short seconds he could move again, and he got up, totally pain-free. Everyone else in the room had just remained frozen where they were until Reinhard got up.

Chapter 22 - A Dream Come True
Back to School

While we lived in that house, when I was fifty-four or fifty-five years old, I fulfilled a twenty-five year dream and went to college. It was one of the reasons I joined the Air Force. I had waited so long after leaving the Air Force that my eligibility expired and I couldn't use the GI bill anymore.

I ended up going to a small two year college in our small town, using some financial aid. I was in seventh-heaven. I didn't have any children at home to take care of, they were all gone now, and I had six to seven classes a day plus lots of homework at night. It was a tough course to finish, but in two years I graduated with honors and had a degree in Graphic Design. I have never been able to do anything with it since I graduated, but as soon as I was finished I said, *"Lord, I put this on the altar for you. It was a dream and now I have fulfilled it. If you want to do something with it then I will do it, if not I will let it die."*

Reinhard surprised me with a graduation gift of a road trip. Just the two of us drove off and ended up going through twenty-two States in twenty-one days and traveling thousands of miles. He preached in a few of those places. It was wonderful. We saw some incredible things along the way. I took him to where I was stationed in New Mexico for four years, and then we saw places even I hadn't been to before, like Mt. Rushmore. It was a very precious time together.

Chapter 23 - Mom or God?
Whom Do I Honor?

We had told my mom that we were getting ready to move out of the country again. She did not want us to go. After eighteen years in Austria, she was finally happy to have us around for a while, even though we were still a nine hour drive away from her. But I was fully determined to follow God and do what he wanted.

And then my mom was diagnosed with stage-four lung cancer. She had smoked for about thirty years of her life, but she had given it up at least twenty years prior to this date. We all went to her house for Thanksgiving, and she had already lost a lot of weight. I told my sister, who lived with my mom, that I would be back to help her take care of Mom after the New Year, of 2014. Now that Mom had cancer, she was really expecting us to stay, but we had still planned to move to Brazil in March.

We were ministering prophetically at a church just before the end of the year, and one of the people we were ministering to was a family counselor, so I asked him for his advice. He said it was a very difficult situation, but I should try to ask Mom for her blessing to release me to move to Brazil. That was what I planned to do. I talked to Mom's pastor in her town and asked him if he would go with me when I talked to her to ask for her blessing. In the end he said I needed to do it alone.

January 2nd I flew up to my mom's house, and my sister was already panicking when I got there because mom was so bad. I told her to calm down because I was there to help her now. I started making fresh pressed juices trying to get my mom to eat better. She would hardly eat anything at all. They had started her on radiation, and after every treatment she got worse. A few days after I got there, she started to become more and more unresponsive. She just basically slept on the couch the whole time. One day she did sit up, but she just kept moaning. I tried to get her to tell us what was wrong, but she wouldn't talk to us.

We ended up taking her to the hospital, and they admitted her immediately, and said that we should not have had to deal with that on our own. On January 6th they put her into hospice care, which is removing all life support and fluids and just making her as comfortable as they could with all the pain medication she wanted so she could go as quickly and painlessly as possible. She died six days later with my sister, Reinhard and me in the room. I had called Reinhard a few days prior and told him that if he wanted to see her again, he would have to come quickly. He did.

We had to have her cremated because it was her wish, and because there was really nothing left of her. We didn't want people to remember her like that. Afterwards Reinhard went home because he had a surgery scheduled for his sinuses. I stayed to help my sister get my mother's financial estate in order because it was a big mess. We had to hire a lawyer and get all the paperwork sorted out. I was there for about a month.

Almost Lost Reinhard

In the meantime, Reinhard had the surgery on his sinuses and was not recovering well. He was home alone, and the doctor had overdosed him on a certain medication. He was having some terrible side effects. We had a nurse friend who dropped by a few times to check on him, and one evening she said he needed to go to the hospital quickly. He said he would be fine.

Shortly after she left Reinhard lost consciousness. He awoke several hours later to someone calling his name, but nobody was there. Later he found out that on that very night three different people, in three different countries, had interceded for him at that very time he passed out. He probably would have died without their intercession. Some other people said to him that there was no way he was going to be able to go to Brazil. He just replied, *"I will go to Brazil in a coffin if it has to be, but I am going."* I had no idea, until later, how bad he actually was.

But in the meantime, the lady who had taken our dog (a different dog than the one in

Austria) for us emailed me to tell me that the dog had either run away or was stolen. The dog was gone for five days then she finally returned to a friendly neighbor's home very near our friend. She had been injured. My friend took her to the veterinarian, and the vet thought that she might have been hit by a car. They gave her some pain pills and antibiotics, and told her to come back on Monday for an X-ray. On Monday they discovered that the dog had been shot, and they had to amputate her leg.

When I came home from being with my sister, I was surprised how everything had turned out. I never had to make the decision to obey God instead of my mother, nor did I have to leave her in such a state. I'm pretty sure that if I had left the country and left my sister alone with my mom that my sister would never have spoken to me again. I would have understood her too. I couldn't explain to her the verse, *"Let the dead bury their own dead; you follow Me."* That was what I kept hearing every time I thought about what I should do, obey God or succumb to Mom's pressure to stay.

Chapter 24 – The Move to Brazil
Front Lines Moving Again

Then came the day in March (my younger son's birthday) (only a father would plan leaving the country on his son's birthday; no mother would ever do that), when we had to leave to move to Brazil. Just prior to my going up to help my sister and mom, I had gone to a veteran's hospital to have a mole removed from my shoulder. They sent it away for testing. We were driving to the city where the airport was, and I called the hospital to get the results of the mole removal. They told me it was cancer, and that I needed to stay out of the sun. I laughed and told them that I was right at that moment on my way to move to a city in Brazil where the sun basically shines all year round. Not to mention that I love the sun!

We had the last lunch with our sons, and then one of them took us to the airport. As he was hugging us good-bye, he suddenly started sobbing and begging us not to move to Brazil, not to leave him there. We had offered to take them with us, but they refused to move to yet another continent. They were happy in the

States and wanted to stay, so this reaction shocked us. Then he said that it was ok, he would be fine, and he drove off. Somebody was pulling out all the stops to try to keep us from moving to Brazil.

We had gone to Brazil a few times previously and had taken a few suitcases each time and left them in Brazil. When we left our home we told all our friends and church family that if they wanted anything they should come to our house and take it for free. Many people came and cleared out everything. That was the exact same thing we did when we left Austria. We didn't try to sell anything. We just gave it all away.

When the Lord had told us to move to the US, we didn't even have the money for the airfare to fly there nor any place to stay once we got there, but we started the preparations in faith. By the time we left the country, about five months later, we had so much money we had to declare it when we were entering the US. And some people that we had only met one time previously, picked us up at the airport and took us to their home for as long as we needed to stay, which ended up to be only four weeks before we rented our own home. And they are now some of our best friends in the States.

What We Witnessed in Brazil

Once in Brazil we were welcomed so warmly and kindly. So many people helped us with so many things, especially because we couldn't communicate when we first arrived. After a few months we went up north to São Luís, Maranhão to do a conference. The things we heard and saw there broke our hearts. We wondered why the Christians weren't doing anything to help the poorest of the poor up there.

After a few months of prayer and thinking, we decided to start orphanages to help the poor children to get off the trash heaps and the streets. The pastors up there came up with a vision, and we were determined to help them. We sent out newsletters to some of our friends explaining the situation and the things we had learned and heard about. Soon people started asking how they could help financially, and funds started to come in, but we never specifically asked anybody for money. We just informed people about what was happening, or what we had seen.

Somebody else offered to make us a website and now it is in four languages. By the way, the website is, ***www.braziliankidskare.org***, in case you are interested in all that we saw and experienced up there and are doing today.

We have also started the adoption process to adopt a child once everything is in order, and we might already have one picked out (a teenage boy – who else?). We are again waiting for the Lord's perfect timing. We are preparing to become parents again. By the time you are reading this we could already have our new child home with us. In the end our goal is to build 100 orphanages in Brazil.

To date we have one Day Care Center in São Luís and one Day Care Center in Natal and an orphanage in Natal as well, all in the north of Brazil. We need a good amount of money every month to sustain the kids and the workers, and God provides everything.

To finish I just want to say that now I finally get to travel a lot with Reinhard. Funny, I joined the Air Force to see the world and ended up in the desert. I let go of my dreams to follow the Lord, and now I am traveling to some of the most amazing places in the world! Jesus says,

> *"And everyone who has left houses or brothers or sisters or father or mother or wife or children or lands, for My name's sake, shall receive a hundredfold, and inherit eternal life."* (Matt. 19:29)

We have left all to follow Jesus, wherever He leads us. And we are ready to keep following Him when He says to move again. Many people ask us how long we will remain in Brazil. Our answer is always the same, *"Until the Lord tells us to move and tells us where to move to,"* or in other words, until the *front lines* move. Sometimes we don't even know where we are going, but we always know Whom we follow and it is always a great adventure.

Made in the USA
Columbia, SC
15 July 2019